Flowering Cacti

a colour guide

G. Rayzer

English translation by Lucia Wildt

DAVID & CHARLES
Newton Abbot London

Photography: Agence Panoramic, Liege, Belgium
Cover photograph: *Echinopsis* x Delrue
Pictogram: Filigrane
Printed by Stabilimento Tipigrafico Ferrero, Romano Canavese

This publication is simultaneously published by:
Kümmerly & Frey, Bern, in German
Daimon Ediciones, Barcelona, in Spanish
Editions Duculot, Paris and Gembloux, in French
Hippocrene Books, New York
Priuli & Verlucca Editori, Ivrea, in Italian

joint members of *club primavera*

British Library Cataloguing in Publication Data

Rayzer, G.
Flowering cacti.
1. Cactus
I. Title II. Guide des cactus en fleurs
English
635.9'3347 SB438

ISBN 0-7153-8602-6

Typeset by Typesetters (Birmingham) Ltd, Smethwick, West Midlands
Printed in Italy

Shape of the spines

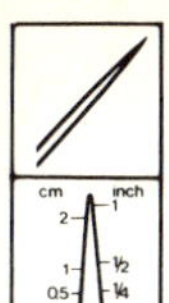

Species with aciculate spines

Average size of the main spines

Disposition and general appearance of the spines

Species with spines growing in star-shaped groups or tufts

Species with long, soft spines giving the plant a woolly appearance

Species with spines growing in feathery tufts

Cultural conditions

Ideal temperatures

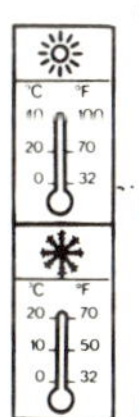

In summer

In winter

Water requirements

In summer: species requiring a very dry soil

In summer: species requiring a slightly moist soil

In summer: species requiring a humid soil

In winter: species requiring a very dry soil

In winter: species requiring a slightly humid soil

In winter: species requiring a humid soil

Ideal lighting conditions

Species flowering well in the sun or in strong light

Species needing half light

Type of soil

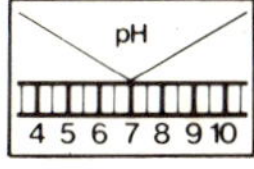

Soil acidity expressed in pH

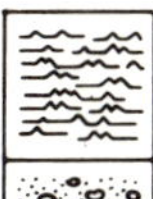

Species to be grown in loamy soil

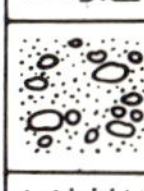

Species to be grown in pebbly and sandy soil

Species to be grown in sandy soil

Species to be grown in 'standard' compost

Possibility of reproduction in cultivation

Germination of seeds difficult or impossible

Germination of seeds easy, giving good results

Grafting: easy, quick recovery

Grafting: difficult, only occasional recovery

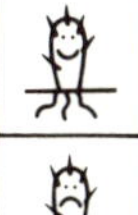

Cuttings: easy, quick development of rootlets

Cuttings: difficult, uncertain results

Diseases and parasites

Species particularly prone to attacks of red-spider mites

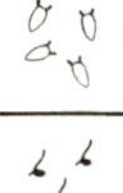

Species particularly prone to attacks of sucking parasites

Species particularly sensitive to nematodes

Species particularly prone to cryptogamic diseases

Longevity

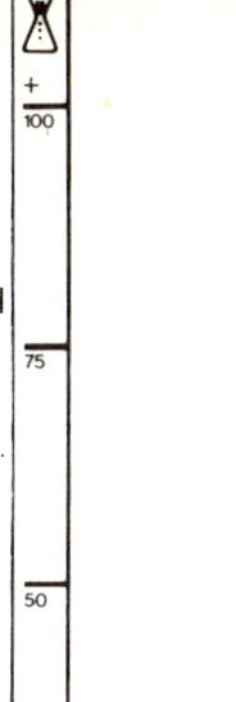

In years

Under each photograph is a symbol showing the general shape of a well-developed specimen in the wild. The size is shown in the table

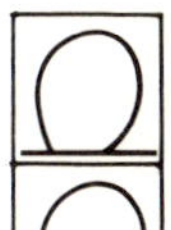

Spherical, globular shape, without shoots

Spherical, globular shape, with lateral shoots

Cespitose shape, with several shoots of varying sizes

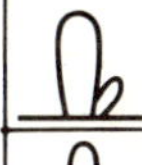

Shape intermediate between globular and candle-like

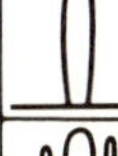

Candle-like shape without ramifications

Candle-like shape with lateral ramifications

Racket-like in shape, occasionally with similarly shaped shoots

Liana-like in shape, frequently with aerial roots

CONTENTS

INTRODUCTION

Cacti are certainly among the strangest plants in the world. The way they have adapted to life in dry areas has caused them to develop extraordinary shapes, dotted with various spines and thorns. Their stark and unusual beauty has attracted collectors and plant amateurs alike, all of whom eagerly await their specimens' flowering time, when glorious blooms appear in a variety of brilliant colours.

This new guide illustrates this extraordinary moment in the life of a cactus with a series of photographs in full colour. Moreover, each illustration is accompanied by a well-tested descriptive system based on a set of clear symbols. Full information on each specimen is thus immediately available, from a detailed description of the parts of the plant to exact instructions as to its culture.

The work represents therefore a mine of useful information not only for the experienced collector, but for the beginner who will be able to discover the world of flowering cacti in all its fascination.

THE DISCOVERY OF CACTI

The discovery of America – of the New World as it was soon called – meant the discovery of an incredible number of strange animals and plants. As the Europeans penetrated to the heart of the continent, new marvels were brought to light; and after the splendour and magnificence of the tropical forests, the explorers were faced with the stark beauty of the deserts. These deserts were not as devoid of life as the Sahara. Here, in the canyons and on the slopes of the rocky hills, strange life forms – the cacti – thrived, sometimes growing in such numbers as to form veritable forests. In the gorges to the north of the area which is now covered by Mexico City, the columnar cereus *(Carnegiea gigantea)* grew to a height of over 15m – thousands of huge living columns, covered in spines, rising amongst the reddish rocks like creatures of a fantastic universe. Other giant species caused a great sensation among the explorers, such as the globular cacti of over a metre in diameter and weighing more than a tonne. These giants grew side by side with dwarf species with a diameter of only a few centimetres.

After the first cursory exploration of this New World by men who were often motivated more by the desire to find gold than by the excitement of scientific discovery, the interest of the true scientists was aroused. Botanists studied the areas in which the various species grew and noted the relationship between the cacti and the native inhabitants. To an Indian, a cactus represented a source of stored water to be used during prolonged drought; nor did he ignore their fruits, particularly those of the so-called prickly pear. But the most important Indian discovery is connected with a chemical compound contained in the flesh of certain cacti, and which affects the brain. The juice of several species contains such hallucinogenic substances. One, called Peyotl by the Indians and *Lophophora* by botanists, contains the hallucinogenic mescaline which affects the sight. Once ingested, it produces visions of brilliant colours and flashing alterations of spatial forms. Aztecs and Toltecs used these cacti during their religious ceremonies and believed they could thus communicate directly with their gods. These rituals, regarded as magic, are still practised by some Indian tribes.

THE SCIENTIFIC APPROACH

The first scientists to explore these regions of the New World were faced with wonder upon wonder, new species upon new species, and they had little time for subtleties. They only recognised and described the larger groups. Hence, while there are thousands of species of

Cactaceae, the first systematical classification worked out by the great Swedish naturalist Carl von Linné in 1758 listed only some twenty species within the genus *Cactus.* Knowledge progressed in steps. In 1768, P. Miller described twenty-eight species in his *Dictionary of Gardening,* and in France that marvellous artist Redouté illustrated *Succulents* by A. P. Candolle (1778-1841) which described over one hundred species.

Noblemen and royalty also took a passionate interest in cacti. At the end of the eighteenth century, the recognised world authority on the subject was Prince J. Salm-Reiferscheid-Dyck who reorganised the systematic taxonomy of the Cactaceae in his two volumes *Hortus Dyckensis* and *Cacteae in horto Dyckensi cultae.* He described over 7,000 species using, as a basis, living specimens from his own collection. He looked after his own botanical garden himself and was in constant touch with other specialists of his day. To crown his life's work he published, at the age of seventy-six, a *Monograph of Aloes and Mesembryanthemum,* which was illustrated by hundreds of splendid engravings.

The cultivation of collections of living cacti was the basis of all scientific research during the nineteenth century, when technical discoveries and new materials allowed the construction of large glasshouses. In England, where technology was more highly developed than in other countries, gigantic glasshouses of over 3,000cub metres were constructed, and hot-water systems were used in winter to heat them and recreate conditions similar to those of the plants' natural habitat. It was thanks to those methods that new species were discovered and described. In Germany, L. Pfeiffer (1805-77) was one such botanist, and towards the end of the century the formation of the German Cacti Society injected new blood into scientific research. Thousands of species were thus re-examined and carefully described by K.M. Schumann in his monumental work *A General Description of Cacti.* The interest in cacti began to diminish, in Europe, at the beginning of the twentieth century; but serious research continued in America where, between 1918 and 1924, the two botanists N. L. Britton and J. N. Rose thoroughly reformed the classification of cacti in their monograph *The Cactaceae.*

Keen amateurs have also abounded in the course of the centuries. At the beginning, only apothecaries, attracted by the plants' strange shapes, were known to cultivate them, but during the sixteenth century certain specimens were grown within the walls of convents. Later, the trend set by the aristocrats was picked up by the middle classes, who started small private collections regularly enriched by cactus-hunters' trips to Mexico or North America. Over the years, hundreds of species were thus introduced into Europe, although the majority died for lack of suitable cultivation methods. The climate of the Mexican deserts or of the Californian hinterland is very difficult to reconstruct artificially, as are the special conditions of the soil. This difficult problem was soon tackled by professional botanists and amateurs alike, but the best techniques were not discovered until much later, when the complete evolution of a plant was closely followed from the very first sprouting of the seed. The conditions necessary for the successful cultivation of cacti were thus gradually discovered, thanks to systematic research, and often with surprising results. It was found, for instance, that it is quite useless to reproduce a 'Mexican desert' within a glasshouse, since certain species develop much more easily and satisfactorily in compost than in sand.

This new method of cultivation has come in the nick of time, for the indiscriminate removal of many cacti from their original habitat has resulted in certain species being seriously threatened. Already rare in their natural environment, their displacement to satisfy market demand has brought them close to extinction; and unless careful steps are taken they will soon join the huge group of vegetable and animal species destroyed by mankind. All collectors have a role to play in this fight for conservation. Firstly, only cultivated species should be sought, and secondly each collection should be enlarged by the judicious exchange of seeds or cuttings. In this way, collecting will give much greater satisfaction, and there will be much greater pleasure from observing the gradual opening of a flower one has raised oneself rather than bought.

This book is aimed at all nature lovers who, because they are interested in the strange world of cacti, will be able to experience something of the excitement of the first explorers and who will, in the peculiar shapes of their plants, recognise the results of adaptations imposed on them by the extreme climatic conditions of the canyons, deserts and mountains of the Americas.

BRIEF BIOLOGICAL NOTES

The desert areas of Mexico, California, Utah, Arizona and New Mexico contain large numbers of cacti species; while in the huge deserts of South America the Cactaceae are definitely the dominant plants. In the Sertao, in north-east Brazil, their growth covers hundreds of square kilometres. They also spread far to the south, in Uruguay, Paraguay, Argentina and Bolivia, and climb to the high plateaux of the Andes where the climate is dry and harsh. Some species are resistant to low temperatures and can be found close to the snow caps. *Oreocereus trollii* thrives at altitudes of over 4,000m; *Tephrocactus floccosus* grows in Peru and can exist at a height of 5,000m. And with each exploration new records are established – a species of *Rebutia* has been found at 5,200m.

The Cactaceae have adapted to life in arid climates characterised by low rainfall, intense heat and sunlight, and extremely dry air. Their adaptation is both morphological (ie affecting their shapes) and physiological (affecting the structure and functioning of their tissues). And if we look at how the species living in extreme environments have adapted, we first of all notice their rounded or barrel-like shape, which allows for maximum volume within a minimum surface area. Secondly, the outer surface consists of a layer of extremely resistant cells impermeable to water and often secreting a kind of wax and it is sometimes covered with long hairs. This bizarre shape presents several advantages with respect to water economy; and the surface with its waxy layer or its hairs, often white, reflects the rays of the sun. The leaves are also reduced and in extreme cases disappear completely, having been transformed into sharp spines.

As in the case of other plants, two vital functions are carried out using the gases contained in the air – respiration, during which oxygen is used and carbon dioxide released; and photosynthesis, which uses carbon dioxide and water to produce sugars. This latter biochemical function is extremely complex and made possible by the presence of chlorophyll: the sun's rays are used as a source of energy. Both these functions requiring the exchange of important gases involve a certain amount of water loss. In order to reduce this, desert cacti breathe mainly at night when the air is cooler, and at the same time 'fix' carbon dioxide within their tissues in the form of various organic acids which are then used in photosynthesis during the day.

Other forms of adaptation are also frequent, such as the roots growing in a bundle on top of the soil. The lightest rainfall, the slightest source of moisture in the top layers of the soil can thus be taken advantage of.

THE FLOWERS THEMSELVES

This guide is entitled *Flowering Cacti,* and it is not by chance that 'flowering' is thus emphasized. Blossoming, so often extremely limited but always touched with grandeur, is a very special time for these plants, the appearance of which is often rendered strange and even aggressive by those hundreds of spines. The brilliantly coloured flowers, which can be admired in the plates section, are reproductive organs; and in order to produce a fruit, the basis of a new plant, they must be fertilised. In the case of cacti, the pollen is transported from flower to flower by animal life be it insects, birds or even bats.

The insects are represented above all by Hymenoptera (bees, wasps, etc) and butterflies. They are attracted by the shape and vivid colours of the flowers as well as by particular smells and substances, such as nectar, which consists of a sugary solution secreted in the depth of the flower. Certain flowers are visited by several kinds of insects, others tend to 'specialise' and open only at night to be fertilised by night moths and butterflies which can hover in front of the flower and unroll their long tongues into its depth. Among the birds, the tiny humming-birds have taken on the role of fertilising certain species of cactus. Since they have practically no sense of smell, they are mainly attracted by flowers with striking colours – vivid red, yellow and orange – and these cacti have therefore no scent at all. But the most striking fertilising agents are the bats, particularly the near relatives of the vampires. They can lick the nectar from the bottom of the calyces with their long tongues and being provided, unlike birds, with an excellent sense of smell, they are attracted by scents. These scents are often disagreeable to humans, but constitute an irresistable attraction for the bats. By visiting the flowers, all these animals – insects, birds and bats – ensure the distribution of the pollen and therefore fertilisation. Their relative or complete specialisation prevents the pollen being wasted on flowers belonging to different species. Like other living creatures, cacti represent millions of years of evolution. The humblest of flowers, the weakest of spines or the most extravagant trunk are the end result of a long history, and of a struggle for life in the most extreme conditions.

PRACTICAL ADVICE

HOW TO ASSEMBLE A COLLECTION

Nowadays, more than ever before, a cactus collector tries to obtain flowering plants. In this connection, it is better to have a small number of plants well looked after and flowering profusely, than a large collection which lack of time or bad choice of species has deprived of proper cultivation and luxuriant growth.

The majority of cacti can be grown without any problems, and a large number of globular or candle-shaped species can produce lovely flowers in record time. But the cultivation rules given below must be followed if the beginner is to build a fine collection of plants in a few years. Let us first distinguish between two types of collections – outdoor collections and indoor collections (raised in glasshouses, homes or cold frames and cloches).

Outdoor collections

Amateurs living in the southern parts of Europe or the United States will have no major problem in establishing a collection or a whole garden of cacti in the open, provided frosts are minimal. Even so, the site should face south-east and, if possible, be slightly raised. If by chance the site is stony, or contains surfacing rocks, so much the better, for a natural habitat will be achieved that much more easily. The soil should be well drained to avoid all stagnant moisture, particularly around the base or the roots of the plants. Ideally the site, once planted, should be covered with sand or gravel, which helps aesthetically as well as in keeping weeds down.

Indoor collections

Collectors living in less favourable areas will have to keep in mind that for at least six months of the year the climate does not encourage the development and flowering of cacti. If they are expected to flower profusely, therefore, their cultivation requirements will have to be attended to as carefully as possible. Very often the amount of heat one can afford will determine the choice of species to be grown.

If only windowsills are available, you should choose robust species needing little light and capable of surviving in special conditions. The selection can include varieties of *Mammillaria, Notocactus, Rebutia* or *Gymnocalycium,* many of which are quite hardy in such situations and capable of flowering when still small. If the room is very dark you will hâve to limit yourself to varieties of *Phyllocactus* or *Zygocactus,* both well-adapted to low-light conditions.

Should a glasshouse be available, the following rules apply:

a If one can maintain a minimum temperature of 10°C or more, certain sub-tropical species such as *Hylocereus* and varieties of *Melocactus, Discocactus, Selenicereus* or *Pilosocereus* can be cultivated without problems. This type of collection is becoming increasingly rare due to the high cost of heating.

b If the heating cannot be more than 8°C, the majority of cacti can still be raised without difficulty.

c If the minimum temperature cannot be raised above 5°C, the choice is more restricted but still offers good possibilities. Best suited will be the genera native to the high plateaux, which are capable of surviving lower temperatures as long as conditions of low humidity are maintained. Among them are varieties of *Echinocereus, Lobivia, Matucana, Oroya* and *Submatucana.*

d A completely cold greenhouse still presents possibilities – certain globular species, such as *Chamaecereus silvestrii, Lobivia titicacaensis, Mediolobivia pygmaea* and some of the *Opuntias.* These can survive freezing temperatures over fairly long periods so long as conditions are kept extremely dry both in terms of compost and atmosphere. If this is done, these species will be covered in buds in the spring.

It must always be remembered that a plant, cactus or otherwise, needs four important elements in order to live and prosper – light, air, heat and humidity. Unlike most other vegetals, the majority of cacti (except for *Rhipsalis, Epiphyllum, Zygocactus* and *Schlumbergera* live in areas with a high ratio of sunlight. Very often, the amount of light they receive at our latitudes is less than that of their natural environment; it is therefore important to be able to give them maximum light, particularly in winter when the days are so short. However, indispensable though light may be to the development of a plant, it can continue to grow in darkness as long as it can rely on sufficient reserves; it will actually grow more quickly because light generates certain substances which prevent the plant from growing too fast. But the epidermis, deprived of light, becomes discoloured, the meristematic centre grows whitish and thin and, if left under these conditions the plant soon perishes. This should be remembered particularly during the overwintering stage when many cacti, like dahlia tubers or potatoes, are plunged for months into darkness; and yet many people are surprised when the nearly deceased specimen, retrieved from the depths in spring, refuses to flower. On the other hand, it should also be remembered that, however much light they may like, cacti still need, at the end of winter, a period of gradual adaptation to direct sunlight.

Those cacti which are natives of the equatorial forests of South America (such as *Rhipsalis, Epiphyllum, Zygocactus* and *Schlumbergera)* adapt very easily to conditions of half shade. If they are kept too long in full sunlight their yellow stems become covered by a dark-red film as a shield against too much light; for the young cells of these plants store up a substance called anthocyanin, which plays the same role as the dark pigmentation of our skin in summer and prevents the young cells from being burnt by the sun's heat. As soon as this phenomenon appears, the plant should be withdrawn from the light and placed in a shadier position.

Air is also very important in the life of a plant as it is from this element that the carbon dioxide necessary to photosynthesis is extracted. Carbon dioxide is required mainly in spring and during the period of full growth, so that collections should be well ventilated then and kept so until the end of autumn, when both ventilation and watering can be decreased. Plants originating from high altitudes require a maximum amount of light and ventilation. Examples are: *Lobivia, Mediolobivia, Oroya, Oreocereus, Matucana* and *Submatucana*.

Heat also plays a dominant role and is indispensable to the great majority of flowering cacti. One could say that the optimum winter temperature should, overall, be around 7° or 8°C. As for the summer temperature, most of these plants are quite happy even when the thermometer soars beyond 40°C, as long as they have enough ventilation.

And, finally, humidity; for unlike numerous indoor plants which require conditions of constant moisture, cacti need a rest period characterised by a marked drop in humidity both in terms of compost and air. This period of more or less intense dryness has a definite effect on the vegetative growth, as well as being necessary to release the flowering mechanism. How many beginners are surprised, at the end of winter, to discover that their favourite plants remain imperturbably sterile, even though they lacked absolutely nothing throughout the dark months – not even water! To sum up: from the end of September, watering must gradually be cut back until only the occasional spraying should be administered in December and January. From late February onwards a little watering should be resumed and gradually increased to reach a maximum during the months of July and August.

CULTIVATION AND PROPAGATION

From seed

It is possible to obtain several species of cacti with little expense by resorting to seeds. The best containers are pots of about 8-10cm diameter or, if large quantities of seed are to be sown, trays of plastic or other materials. All containers should have been properly washed and disinfected, either with potassium permanganate or with a proprietary fungicide. Sufficient drainage should be provided to ensure that no stagnant moisture remains in the pots, which should be filled with compost up to about 1cm from the top. The choice of compost is very important as it will, to a large extent, influence all vegetative growth. Seed compost must not be too rich in nutrients and should preferably be slightly on the acid side. The following mixture can be recommended: one-third river sand (in preference to quarried sand, the granules of which are too fine and produce too compact a mixture); one-third well rotted leaf mould (this is very important, as a compost which is too young and not rotted down enough contains cryptogams which will soon destroy the young seedlings); one-third non-fibrous peat. One should also add a preventive fungicide and steam sterilisation if possible is strongly recommended in order to destroy insect larvae and the dormant seeds of weeds.

A few preliminary operations are recommended. It is advisable for instance to disinfect the seeds in a solution of permanganate of potash before sowing them. Sometimes the seeds are still surrounded by the flesh of the fruit which contained them; this is often sugary and encourages the growth of mildews and rot which would soon destroy the young seedlings. Such seeds should therefore be dried and cleaned before being soaked in the disinfectant solution.

Some seeds are protected by a very hard shell, as in the case of certain *Opuntia* species. They take a few weeks to germinate, sometimes even a few months. Quicker germination can be obtained by soaking them in lukewarm water for a few hours or by immersing them in a solution of 40 per cent sulphuric acid for two or three minutes. The protective shell will thus be partially destroyed and moisture will more easily reach the germ and start the process of germination. Other seeds, such as those of the *Tephrocactus* originating from the high plateaux of the Andes, need a period of hibernation, that is of freezing temperatures, before they can germinate. This is easily achieved by placing them in the freezing compartment of a refrigerator some eight days before they are due to be sown.

The following rules apply to the actual sowing of the seeds:

— The seeds should be sparingly spread over the surface of the compost in order not to impede the development of the seedlings. The operation can be facilitated by the use of a sheet of paper folded in half and used as a funnel – a method which will be found all the more handy when dealing with minute seeds, such as those of the *Blossfeldia* and *Parodia*.

— When sowing larger seeds, one should cover them with a thin layer of sand which will maintain heat and dryness around the seedlings.

Three factors – air, heat and humidity – are essential for germination. Immediately after sowing and until germination occurs, the seed-trays can be kept unventilated with an optimum temperature of about 25°C, never more than 35°C as this would considerably delay germination and growth. Humidity, on the other hand, should be very high. A very simple method of achieving these conditions is to sow the seeds in a pot, soak this with water and then place it in a plastic bag with the opening sealed by an elastic band. The water cycle will thus be blocked, and there will hardly be any evaporation at all. This method offers the additional advantage of needing no attention at all until the seedlings need pricking out. If all these conditions have been met, germination will be very rapid, so that within a couple of days the first seedlings of *Frailea* will be showing, the other species needing generally between two and four weeks.

Once germination has taken place a fourth very important factor, light, is needed. The seedlings must be placed in full light, but should be sheltered with a piece of transparent paper from too hot or too direct sunlight. They tiny cacti are now extremely fragile and can easily die of sunstroke!

As soon as the seedlings begin to grow, humidity should be reduced and ventilation progressively increased. One should also keep a watch for the first signs of mildew which often proliferates on the empty seed shells. Should this appear, they should immediately be removed and a fungicidal treatment carefully carried out. Occasionally, green or brownish algae appear on the surface of the compost, impeding the growth of the seedlings. This indicates the presence of too much lime. If at all possible, it would be better to prick out the young plants into a new and more acid compost but, should they be too small, one can spray the tray with a solution of copper sulphate (1g per litre of water) or sulphuric acid (two or three drops per litre of water).

Generally speaking, pricking out is best carried out when days are warm and sunny, as this will encourage the formation of new roots. The seedlings should be put into pots containing one-third sand, one-third well rotted leaf mould and one-third good loam, the whole having been well sieved. After a few weeks, one can apply a fertiliser based on potash and phosphates as these two chemicals encourage photosynthesis, improve the quality of the plant tissues and their ability to store up nutrients.

It should not be forgotten that in their first year the young cacti do not stop growing in winter so that, more than the other plants in one's collection, they will need as much light as possible during the shorter and darker months. Certain species, such as *Frailea, Rebutia* and *Weingartia,* can flower in their second year, or even during the very first year if they are grafted, very early on, onto specimens of *Peiresthiopsis.*

Cuttings

Several cacti produce shoots which can be very easily used as cuttings – a technique which offers several advantages. First of all, one can quickly and cheaply obtain a large number of young plants which do sometimes flower in the same year. Furthermore, the new plants will have the same characteristics as the mother plant from which they were taken. Cuttings are used to propagate species the seeds of which are virtually unobtainable, or species which have almost disappeared. Occasionally, one can thus prevent a diseased plant from dying. An old plant, or one obviously exhausted, can also be successfully propagated by taking cuttings.

The best time to carry out this operation is from late spring to the end of summer, while the plant is in full vegetative growth. Some 'emergency' cuttings can, however, be carried out in winter, for instance to save a plant attacked by rot. In such cases, the cuttings should be very carefully looked after, since their development will be much more difficult.

Advice which applies to all cacti cuttings, is that one should always choose healthy well-nourished shoots unaffected by chlorosis or parasites – weak cuttings would find it very difficult to root. It should also be noted that a healthy plant usually roots in the middle of the cut surface, at least to begin with; that is why the base of the cutting should be shaped like a cone without the centre being affected. This is particularly so in the case of cuttings taken from cylindrical or globular species. When dealing with flattened types such as *Opuntia* or *Phyllocactus,* one should make diagonal cuts on both sides in order to attract the maximum amount of sap to the lowest part of the plant and to avoid the formation of a cavity where moisture may gather and encourage rot. The cuts themselves should be clean, and sharp tools (grafting knives, pruning knives or scalpels) should always be used, the blade having been previously disinfected. Secateurs or scissors should be avoided even if very sharp, as they invariably damage some of the tissues thus making rooting that much more difficult and opening the door to disease.

After being taken, the cuttings should be dipped in charcoal powder or daubed with a solution of mercury, these two substances having healing properties. They should then be left in a half-shady spot, protected from any trace of moisture, until the cuts have completely healed. This may take three to five weeks. The next stage is to try and get the cuttings to root, and for this one can use rooting powders, either sprinkled on the base of the cutting or incorporated in the compost. The cuttings should then be inserted in pots or trays containing sand and peat in equal parts. The rooting process can be speeded by covering the container with glass or plastic, thus creating an encouragingly stuffy atmosphere. Sufficient shade should be provided on sunny days to avoid sun scorching.

In the case of certain species, such as many *Opuntia,* the fruits can be very successfully treated as cuttings. Green fruits should be used and, once rooted, they will produce shoots identical to those of the mother plant.

Grafting

Certain species of cacti are rather difficult to grow on their own roots, which may be badly affected by the moisture in the soil. Others grow very slowly or hardly flower at all. Grafting can solve these problems; it can also save a plant which has been attacked by some disease; and it is worth noting that, notwithstanding what is often said, grafting does not alter either the plant's shape or the colour of the flowers. As applies to cuttings, grafting can only be successfully carried out during the period when the plants are fully vegetative and the environmental temperature can be maintained at a minimum of 20°C.

The first thing to do when grafting is to make sure that one has suitable stock available: robust and vigorous plants should be chosen, capable of providing all the nutrients which are necessary for the scion to grow. If globular or cereiform plants are to be grafted, the following stocks should be given preference: *Cereus peruvianus, C. validus, C. forbesi, Trichocereus spachianus, T. pachanoi, T. bridgesii, T. macrogonus* and *Eriocereus jusbertii. Echinopsis* species and hybrids can also be used as stock, but they will provide only temporary grafts, the operation having to be repeated within a few years. Dwarf *Opuntia* such as *tephrocactus, maihuenia* and *micropuntia* can be grafted onto *Opuntia ficus-*

indica, O. velutina or *Austrocylindropuntia subulata.* Young seedlings can be grafted onto *Pereskiopsis,* and this particular operation is dealt with below.

Grafting techniques are relatively simple. The top of the stock should be cut off horizontally, making sure the tissues are neither too young nor too woody and that the edges of the cut are bevelled, as the centre of the plant may otherwise develop a dip. Should this happen, the join between scion and stock would have a gap, with highly dubious results. The scion should be kept in place by permanent gentle pressure, using a weight or an elastic band, for several days, until the tissues have properly welded. Grafts of *Rhipsalis* or *Zygocactus* can be carried out using the wedge method as follows:

— the top part of the stock should be cut to a point
— the lower part of the scion should be incised accordingly
— the two areas should be made to adhere perfectly.

The plants should be kept in place with a spine of *Opuntia* or *Pereskia,* never with a pin which would soon rust and cause rapid deterioration of the plant tissues and consequent rotting. Once the grafting has become established, the development of lateral shoots on the stock should be prevented, as they would only grow to the detriment of the scion. After about a month, the grafted plant can be treated like all the other plants in the collection.

A special kind of graft – the one practised on *Pereskiopsis* – is used only in the case of young seedlings particularly those which appear to be fragile, or the rarer ones as by this method they can be more easily saved. *Pereskiopsis* is a cactus with slightly crassulescent leaves and successful cuttings can be taken from the beginning of May. After three weeks, the cuttings will have rooted enough to be potted on separately in standard compost and individual pots of about 7cm diameter. The new plants can be used as stock any time after mid July; they should be placed in a warm place (25°C minimum) with an enclosed and humid atmosphere.

Three weeks before, one should have sown the seeds required, and it is these seedlings which will be grafted onto the young *Pereskiopsis.* The technique is relatively simple. The tops of the stock plants should be cut horizontally, and a seedling, cut horizontally just above the roots, should be placed on the cut. It is very important, in this case, that the scion should be quite simply deposited onto the stock, without any pressure or support being used. This kind of grafting should be carried out in situ to avoid moving the plants and displacing the scions, and the trays should be kept in the shade. After a few weeks, the grafts should take and the young plants should henceforward prosper.

GENERAL CARE

Choosing the compost

Choosing the compost is extremely important as it is one of the essential elements in the success of all future operations. The basic considerations influencing this choice have been radically altered over the past few years. Once, plants used to be placed in composts formed almost entirely of sand, highly alkaline and poor in nutrients. Today, as a result of further research and experiments with the soil itself, the procedure is quite different; and the majority of cacti are cultivated in a 'standard' compost made up of one-third sand (river sand is preferred to quarry sand, which is too fine and compacts too easily), one-third well rotted and sifted vegetable mould, and one-third sifted soil.

A factor to watch is the acidity of the compost itself, which is expressed by the pH and represented by a number between 0 and 14 showing the ratio acidity/alkalinity. The pH is the logarithm of the ionic concentration of ion H^+ in a water solution. For instance, if $H^+ = 1/1000$, ie 10^{-3}, the pH is 3. A pH 7 is neutral; between 7 and 0 the acidity increases; between 7 and 14, the alkalinity increases. As a general rule, all vegetal organisms can only survive in a pH between 3 and 9, but as far as the cacti are concerned the ideal pH is around 6. To measure this pH, all one has to do is to immerse a small, homogeneous part of the compost in question into distilled water and leave it there for a few hours. A specially prepared piece of paper dipped into the liquid will then change colour according to the degree of acidity or alkalinity of the solution and, by comparing the colour of the paper with a colour scale, one will know the pH. If the compost is too alkaline one can add peat or sulphates, such as iron sulphate; if it is too acid, one should add some bone meal.

While the majority of cacti need a slightly acid compost, some of them easily adapt to more alkaline ones – for instance *Ariocarpus, Strombocactus* and certain *Astrophytum* species. Some cacti have napiform roots, ie resembling small turnips. Should one wish to avoid grafting them in order to maintain this characteristic, extra care should be taken with drainage when potting them on. It would be advisable, in this connection, to spread small gravel or coarse river sand all round the base of the plant. Above all, and particularly if the plant is to be grown in the open soil, extra drainage should be provided immediately below the roots, in the form of crushed crocks.

The best water to use

Choosing the water is also something which should be done very carefully. It should always be clear, limpid, without smells, and preferably acid to neutral. Rain water or river water should be used, the latter only if one can be certain that it is not polluted or does not run over calcareous layers. Tap water should be avoided as it too often contains additives.

Fertilisers

Research carried out at the Jardin Exotique in Monaco has shown that, in their natural state, the great majority of cacti lived on soils rich in nutrients such as potash and phosphates. Let us therefore look at the role which these chemicals play in the well-being of plants. Potash facilitates the production of chlorophyll and the formation of reserve tissues; phosphates are particularly important in furthering the flowering and fruiting of a plant. Nitrogen is also very important, as it is the main element affecting vegetative growth. All three fertilisers should therefore be applied and we recommend the following proportions: 26 per cent potash (sulphate or nitrate of potash), 20 per cent phosphates (super-phosphates) and 10 per cent nitrogen (sulphate or nitrate of ammonia).

The best time to apply fertilisers is during the growing period, between May and September, and frequent but weak applications are to be preferred to strong but infrequent ones. Unless they are used properly, fertilisers are a double-edged weapon; for excessive doses can produce the phenomenon called exosmosis, involving a higher concentration of mineral salts in the water than in the roots. As a result, the water contained in the roots seeps out into the compost towards the higher concentration of salts, thus causing an often fatal dehydration of the plant. It is advisable, in order to minimise the risk of exosmosis, to soak the plants generously with clear water the day before watering them with the fertilising solution.

THE ENEMIES OF CACTI

Suctorial parasites

Red-spider mites

Distant relations of the spiders, these creatures are some of the worst enemies of cacti as they are hardly visible to the naked eye, being no bigger than ¼ mm. Attacked plants become tinged with lead grey or rusty brown, particularly on the surface of the younger tissues. Their presence can also be detected by the numerous tiny webs they weave along the veins or among the spines, sometimes in the centre of the areolae. They reproduce themselves very quickly, especially in a warm and dry environment. Treatment can be:

— **Preventive:** the atmospheric humidity should be maintained sufficiently high, particularly in dry periods, by frequent overhead spraying.

— **Remedial:** attacked plants should be separated from the rest of the collection. Treat with insecticide or acaricide, either by spraying or dusting; acaricides have been specifically formulated for the destruction of these pests. The operation should be repeated every fortnight to ensure that all the parasites have been killed.

Scale insects

These creatures vaguely resemble a tiny woodlouse but are entirely white. Their minute eggs are covered in a white, cottonwool-like fur. They are also to be reckoned with as they multiply rapidly and cause irreparable damage to the epidermis of the cacti.

— **Preventive treatment:** spraying or dusting with insecticides.

— **Remedial treatment:** in the event of a serious infestation, a systemic insecticide should be used, capable of being assimilated by all the plant's cells. The operation should be repeated after a fortnight since the eggs, protected by their woolly coating, are difficult to destroy.

Kermes

These insects resemble tiny cones, round or elongated, with rounded apex, brown or whitish when young, and rather waxy.

— **Preventive treatment:** as for scale insects.

— **Remedial treatment:** their very structure makes these insects very difficult to eliminate. If only a few plants are affected, they can easily be sprayed with a 50 per cent solution of surgical spirit; otherwise it would be better to use an insecticide, even a systemic one in the case of serious infestation.

Root mealy bugs

These are whitish, oval larvae about 3mm to 5mm long. It is difficult to detect their presence as they live on the lower parts of the plants, hidden in the soil, and it is therefore necessary to remove the plant from the pot in order to find them. They attack mainly the young roots and proliferate in a compost which has been allowed to dry out too much.

— **Preventive treatment:** use a compost which is not too porous, and keep it sufficiently moist, particularly during the period of vegetative growth.

— **Remedial treatment:** thoroughly clean the roots and bathe them in an alcoholic solution. Repot the plants after adding a soil insecticide to the compost.

Gnawing parasites

The damage caused by these predators is characterised by bites on the surface of the tissues.

Woodlice

These can easily be destroyed by using bait such as potatoes or, in the case of serious attack, a soil insecticide.

Snails and slugs

These creatures are particularly active at night, and it is easy to see whether they have been around or not because they leave a slimy transparent track on the soil. They can easily be disposed of by placing a proprietary brand of slug pellets among the plants. The operation will have to be repeated several times as, once moistened, the pellets loose much of their effectiveness.

The sciarid fly

Its tiny larvae (1-3mm) can cause great damage mainly by biting the base of the plants and the upper roots. They live in the moulds of composts and look like small, transparent caterpillars with a black head. Their small size makes them difficult to detect, so that one has to keep an eye open for the adult insect – a small fly about 2mm long. The adults can be killed with any insecticide or fly spray, while a soil insecticide or a systemic spray can be used against the larvae.

Other pests

Sometimes earthworms can be found inside moist pots. They do not attack the plants directly but can damage the roots, sometimes noticeably retarding the growth of the plant. Their presence is given away by the small mounds of wet soil broken down to tiny glomerules which appear on the surface of the compost. They can be got rid of by re-potting the plant or by raising the temperature of the pot to 25°C. Should the plants be grown in the open, one can use specially formulated products – a soil drench containing malathion is usually recommended.

Sometimes, in winter, ants may try to colonise a cacti collection. They are particularly fond of the flowers and buds, upon which they feed; and they also attack the fruits, which they store in their tunnels. A proprietory product will soon get rid of them, or one could place in their path the leaves of tomatoes and tagetes, the smell of which they detest.

The nematodes

These are probably the most dangerous of all the enemies of cacti. They are microscopic worms which penetrate the root tissues and are therefore that much more difficult to detect, since one is aware of their presence only when they are already well established. However, it is the plants cultivated in the open which are particularly prone to their attacks. They symptoms indicating such an attack of nematodes are an almost total lack of growth, no flowering, a discoloration of the epidermis which becomes gradually yellowish, and the appearance of cysts of varying dimensions on the roots.

— **Preventive treatment:** while there is hardly any preventive treatment as such, it is always a good idea to avoid leaving old roots in the soil or on the plants when these are being re-potted. 'Old roots' are all underground organs without rootlets or which obviously consist of dead tissues.

— **Remedial treatment:** a specially formulated product should be used, but with great care as it can be dangerous. All attacked roots should be cut off and burnt. Contaminated soil should also be burnt.

Diseases

Wet moulds

These attack, above all, young seedlings or cuttings which have been put down to root too soon. This type of mould is caused by a fungus and often attacks the base of a plant; it gradually spreads over the rest, so that the watery tissues quickly become a blackish, nauseous mass. Action should be taken as soon as the first symptoms are observed, particularly in the case of plants in the open or in trays where the mycelium can, in a matter of a few days, gain much ground and attack still healthy roots. Diseased plants should be burnt together with the contaminated compost, and all the others should be sprayed with a fungicide.

Dry moulds
The presence of these is indicated by the appearance of small rusty spots on the surface of the plant; in winter, these spots are covered by a whitish film. Such fungi are rather difficult to control, so much so that in many cases the plant attacked has to be trimmed back. Exposure to the sun seems to be the only preventive measure.

Deficiencies and chlorosis

Occasionally, otherwise healthy cacti develop a yellowish appearance, due either to an imbalance in the pH or to the compost's being too acid or, more likely, too alkaline. In such cases, the pH can be put right by re-potting the specimen or by watering correctly (see page 18).

Should the pH be correct, the yellowing may be due to the scarcity or lack of a certain trace element: the nutritional balance can then be rectified by the application of a complete fertiliser containing all trace elements.

PROTECTING ENDANGERED SPECIES

The number of cactus collectors has been growing steadily since the end of World War II, particularly in industrialised countries such as Belgium, Great Britain, the Netherlands, Japan, Mexico and the United States. The plants have therefore been gathered in increasingly larger numbers, in an effort to satisfy the growing infatuation with cacti and succulents in general. The number of plants wrenched from their natural habitat is increasing every year, bringing the acquisition of imported varieties well within the reach of more and more purses. And collectors have gradually become more and more demanding, often vying with one another in the effort to assemble excessively large collections.

The majority of plants coming onto the market tend to be rare, of slow growth, and often from a very limited natural habitat. Yet, each year, thousands of plants are uprooted, both in North and South America, and sent to the four corners of the world. Obviously, the plants thus removed from the heart of a natural colony are always the most beautiful, the healthiest, and those which are free of parasites and other faults. It follows that a site thus plundered will often be left only with second-rate specimens, less well adapted and less resistant. Some plants already rare are now almost unique; but still they are being roughly grubbed up, though many will never make it to the end of the journey to their windowsill or greenhouse. It should also be noted that an imported plant introduced into a collection often stops growing, or grows deformed and, generally speaking, flowers much less profusely than an individual of the same species growing in its own habitat where it iswell adapted to the particular environmental conditions.

It is essential that collectors should become aware of the gravity of this situation for a future which is perhaps only a few decades away; also that to acquire an imported plant is to assume responsibility for one of the supports of the natural heritage of our planet.

With a little practice, the collector will soon realise that by starting with a few seedlings grafted onto *Pereskiopsis* he can soon obtain an almost adult plant which, the following year, can be grafted onto its definitive stock (eg *Trichocereus).* Two or three years after sowing, these plants will be able to flower and more than replace any imported ones in the collection – imported ones which could never really prosper. It is in cases like these that the importance of botanical gardens lies; for here threatened and disappearing species can be cultivated, propagated and multiplied. Certain private institutions have also greatly helped this cause. The ISI (International Succulent Institute) for instance offers cuttings, seedlings and graftings of rare and threatened cacti and succulents, all at very reasonable prices. And in the United States it is against the law to collect species on the endangered species list of the Interior Departments' Fish and Wildlife Service.

HOW TO PHOTOGRAPH YOUR SPECIMENS

While it is obvious that not many amateurs can have at their disposal the kind of professional apparatus which was used to take the photographs appearing in this book, it is also true that good snapshots of one's own plants are not impossible. The quality of the final results will depend on the photographer as much as on the equipment used. Anyone wishing to obtain a good picture in which the plant does not appear as a greenish mass closer to a cauliflower than to the original, should follow these simple rules:

1 *Be careful about the distance:* if your camera allows it, focus the plants with precision; if the model you use is very basic, with fixed focus, do not get too close to your subject – generally speaking the minimum distance allowed by such cameras is 1.5m, so don't get any closer. If you operate a reflex camera, don't forget that, while focussing is easier, the closer you get to the subject the less is the depth of field. To avoid a flat image you will have to use a diaphragm: you will therefore need a lot of light, or the image will be blurred.

2 *Isolate your subject:* if the plant is on a cupboard, there is no need to show everything around it; get rid of the background and surroundings. It is the plant that must show up on the photograph, so think of all possible means to underline its beauty.

3 *The exposure must be correct:* if your camera cannot control the exposure don't think you can't do anything about it. If the room you are in is too dark your photo will be poor: don't hesitate to use flash, but beware of glass, mirrors and other reflecting surfaces.

If you can control the exposure, you will still find it is a good idea to take several pictures with different apertures and then have only the best one printed.

4 *Avoid blur:* at short distances and in room lighting, it is easy for a photo to come out blurred because of faulty focussing and a sudden movement. It is definitely advisable to use a tripod or other means of support.

5 *Example:* if your plant is large it will be very easy to obtain a good picture by photographing it in its usual place in front of the window: its shape will stand out against the light and, should the outdoor light be too bright, the use of flash will help to avoid ending up with just a dark shape. But don't forget to open the window to avoid reflections.

6 *Miscellaneous:*
Don't forget to put a film in your camera – you'd be surprised how often this happens, and not only to others!

— be careful about spines; some of them can cause very painful infections, so take precautions.
— quite apart from all the technical advice which can be given, never forget that you are photographing *your* plant to *your* satisfaction and the way *you* see it. Look at it, then take your time over the focussing, lighting etc, so that your chances of success will be that much greater.

How the photographs in this book were taken

Several different techniques were used to take these pictures of flowering cacti. First of all, the demands of the project meant the use of 24 x 36 format material and cameras of current type (Minolta SRT 100X, Minolta XE5 and Asahi Pentax Spotmatic). We chose macro objectives of 50 and 100mm. As we wished to obtain perfect definition, we would have preferred to use Kodachrome film, but since flowering time is extremely brief and we wished to be able to process the photographs immediately, we could not wait for laboratory results. Hence Ektachrome 64 was used for the majority of the pictures.

Since the aim of the photographs was to show the beauty of the flowers as well as the particular characteristics of cacti, eg the spines, we decided to employ a softer version of the 'against the light' technique. The main lighting, coming from a three-quarter's angle, enhances the flowers and underlines the shape of the plant, while the light coming from behind makes the spines stand out to advantage.

Whenever possible, we used artificial lighting in order to be able to exercise maximum control over lighting effects. Equipment varied from a portable flash Braun F 800 Pro to studio material Broncolor with Quadroflex reflector. Measurement was obtained with a Sixtron flashmeter and a Lunasix 3.

We avoided intrusive backgrounds as far as possible, by isolating the subject from its surroundings with backdrops of coloured paper, even when photographing plants in the open. The photographs took several years to shoot. Each flower was photographed on several occasions, each time with modifications in the lighting and diaphragms; this enabled us to exploit the film to best advantage.

HOW TO READ THE SYMBOLS

1 THE SCOPE OF THE PICTOGRAMS

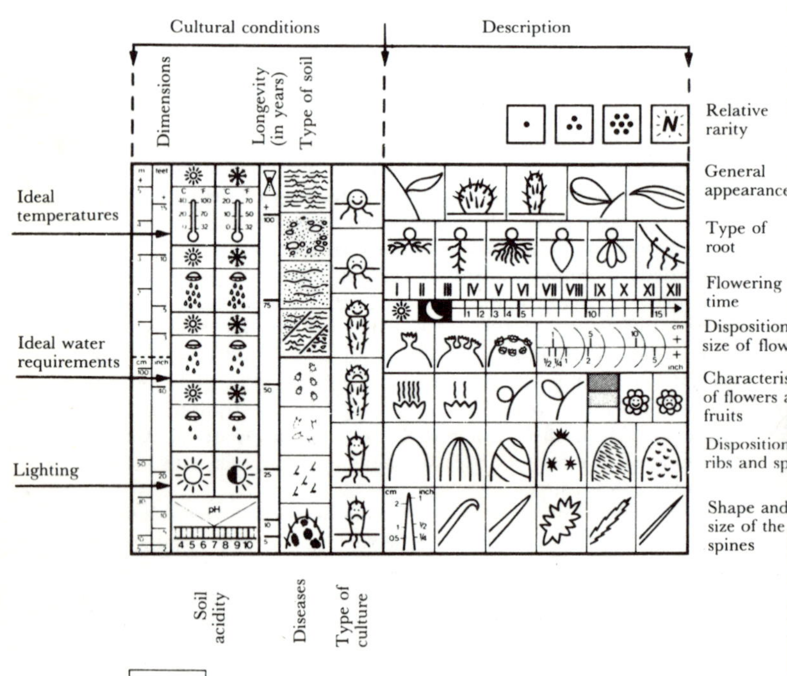

General appearance of an adult specimen in its natural habitat

2 DESCRIPTION AND MEANING OF THE SYMBOLS

a relative rarity

Rare species; must not be collected in the wild.

Fairly common species.

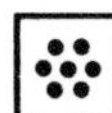

Common species; abundant in the wild and/or easy to propagate in cultivation.

A species newly introduced into cultivation; usually a horticultural variety selectively obtained; more rarely a species only recently described.

b dimensions

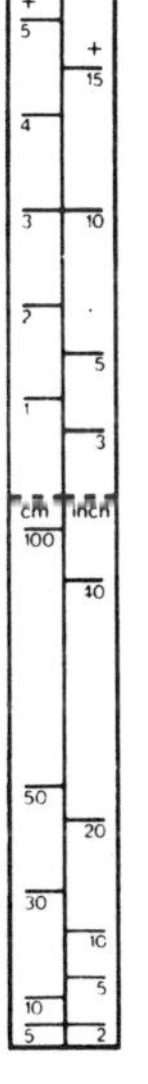

Dimensions of a well-developed adult specimen in the wild. Dimensions of cacti vary considerably according to the species, so that two scales have to be used:
— left, scale for species no taller than 100cm/40in
— right, scale for species taller than 1m/3ft
All dimensions are of course approximate and depend on local conditions.

c general appearance

Species with clearly visible leaves growing on the main stem.

Compact species, rounded or cylindrical, with more or less developed spines.

Candle-shaped species, even when young, with more or less developed spines.

Oval species.

Species with many leaves and very few spines.

d types of root

Species with a system of superficial roots never reaching very dee into the soil.

Species with deep taproot descending vertically into the soil.

Species with fasciculated roots, forming a network of several rootlets

Species with a large napiform root, ie in the shape of a turnip.

Species with tuberous roots growing in large clumps.

Species with aerial roots growing on the stem and stretching progressively towards the soil.

e disposition of the flowers

Isolated flower.

Grouped flowers.

Flowers growing in a circle on top of the plant.

f size of the flowers

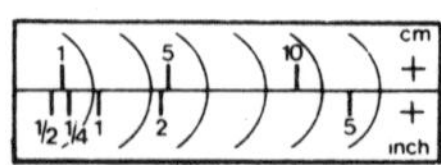

Diameter of fully open flowers: cm (above) and inches (below).

g flowering characteristics

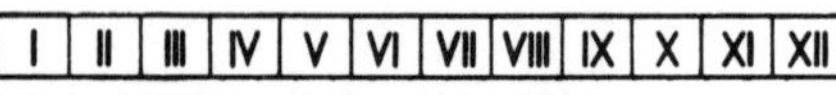

Flowering time (month).

1 2 3 4 5 10 15

Duration of the flowers (in days).

Daytime flowering.

Nocturnal flowering.

Flowers with very faint scent or none at all.

Scented or very scented flowers.

Species producing abundant flowers very easily.

Species does not flower easily and is very sensitive to cultural and environmental conditions.

h characteristics of fruits

Species with globular rounded fruits.

Species with elongated fruits.

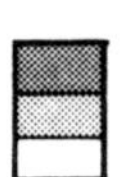

Colour of the fruits: reddish-brown
yellow
transparent

i disposition of the ribs

Species with very faint ribs or no ribs at all.

Species with parallel ribs.

Species with spiralling ribs.

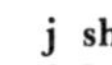

j shape of the spines
NB. Several different types of spines can be present on any given species.

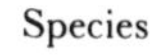

Species with hooked spines.

Species with smooth spines.

Species with pectinate spines on either side of a central line.

Species with finely barbed spines.

Species with aciculate spines, ie long and thin.

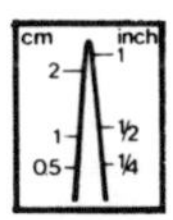

Average size of the main spines: left, in cm
right, in inches.

k disposition and general appearance of the spines

Species with spines growing in star-shaped groups or tufts.

Species with long, soft spines giving the plant a woolly appearance

Species with spines growing in feathery tufts.

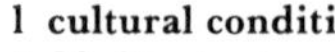

l cultural conditions

1 *Ideal temperatures*

In summer: left, in Centigrade
right, in Fahrenheit.

In winter: left, in Centigrade
right, in Fahrenheit.

2 *Water requirements*

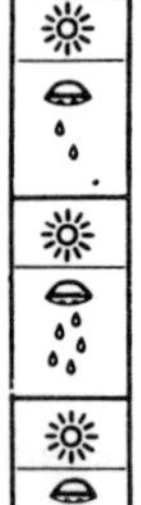

In summer: species requiring a very dry soil; water requirements very reduced; in the majority of cases it is enough to water once a month.

In summer: species requiring a slightly moist soil. Limited need for water; in the majority of cases it is enough to water once a week

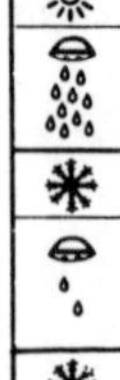

In summer: species requiring a humid soil; the need for water is important and the plant should be watered daily.

In winter: species requiring a very dry soil; water requirements very reduced; usually enough to water once a month.

In winter: species requiring a slightly humid soil; limited water requirements – it is usually enough to water once a week.

In winter: species requiring a humid soil; watering is important and should be done daily.

3 *Ideal lighting conditions*

Species flowering well in the sun or in strong light.

Species needing half light.

4 *Type of soil*

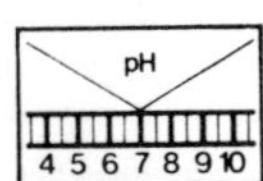

Soil acidity expressed in pH.

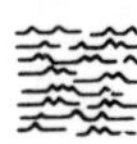

Species to be grown in loamy soil.

Species to be grown in pebbly and sandy soil.

Species to be grown in sandy soil.

Species to be grown in 'standard' compost: ⅓ soil, ⅓ sand, ⅓ vegetal compost, roughly mixed.

5 *Possibility of reproduction in cultivation*

Germination of seeds difficult or impossible.

Germination of seeds easy, giving good results.

Grafting: easy, quick recovery.

Grafting: difficult, only occasional recovery.

Cuttings: easy, quick development of rootlets.

Cuttings: difficult, uncertain results.

6 *Diseases and parasites*

Species particularly prone to attacks of red-spider mites.

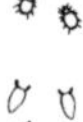

Species particularly prone to attacks of sucking parasites.

Species particularly sensitive to nematodes (tiny worms developing in the soil).

Species particularly prone to cryptogamic diseases brought about by fungi.

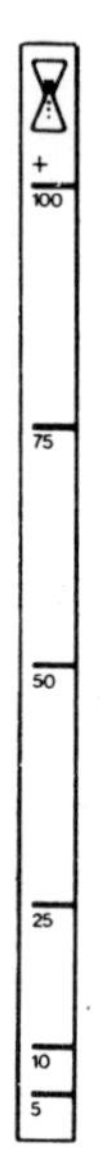

In ideal cultural conditions, the longevity of a species is expressed in years. In the case of new species or horticultural varieties, the longevity is obviously unknown.

Under each photograph is a symbol showing the general shape of a well-developed specimen in the wild. The size is shown in the table.

Spherical, globular shape, without shoots.

Spherical, globular shape, with lateral shoots.

Cespitose shape, with several shoots of varying sizes.

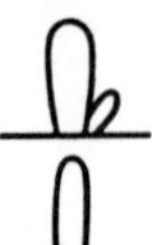

Shape intermediate between globular and candle-like, with occasional lateral shoots.

Candle-like shape without ramifications.

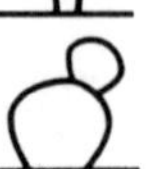

Candle-like shape with lateral ramifications.

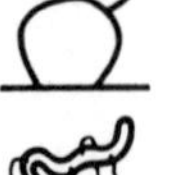

Racket-like in shape, occasionally with similarly shaped shoots.

Liana-like in shape, frequently with aerial roots.

1

Austrocylindropuntia salmiana (Parm.) Backbg.

Argentina, Bolivia

2

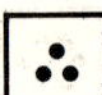
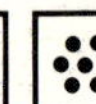

Aztekium ritteri (Böd.) Böd.
Mexico

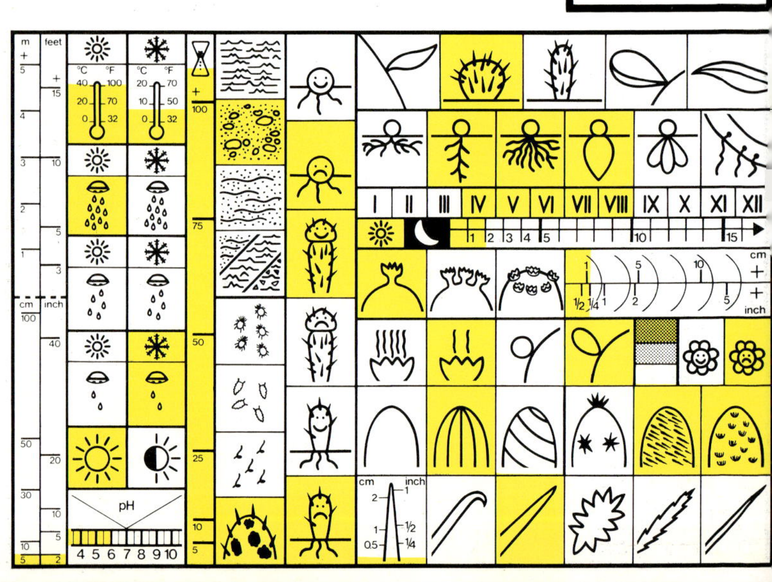

Blossfeldia liliputana Werd.
var. **atroviridis** Ritt.
Argentina

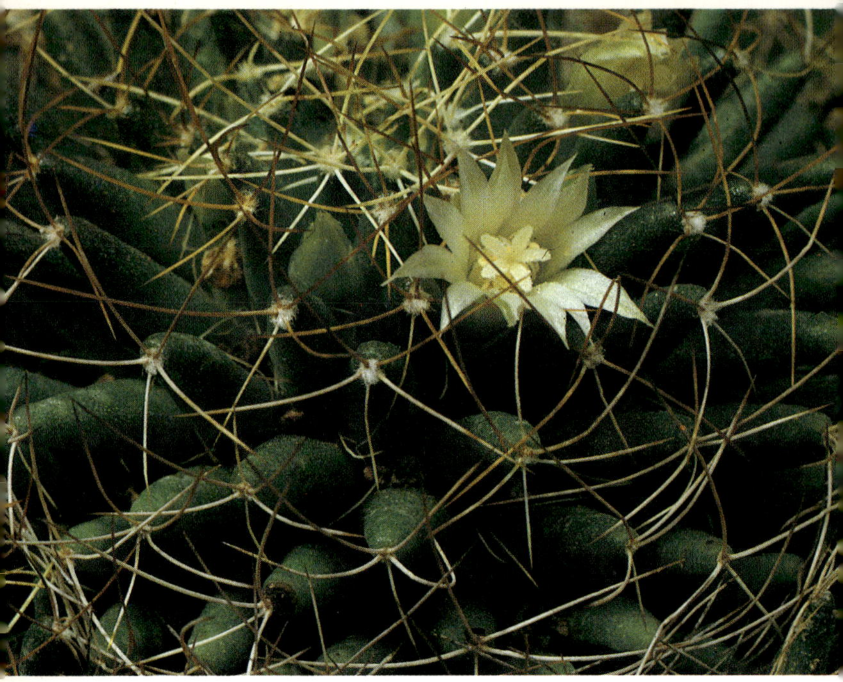

Dolichothele albescens (Tieg.) Backbg.
Mexico

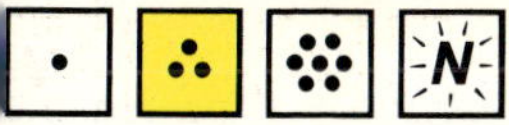

Echinopsis ayopayanus Card.
Bolivia

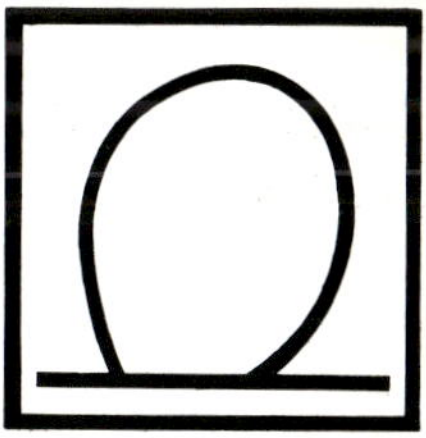

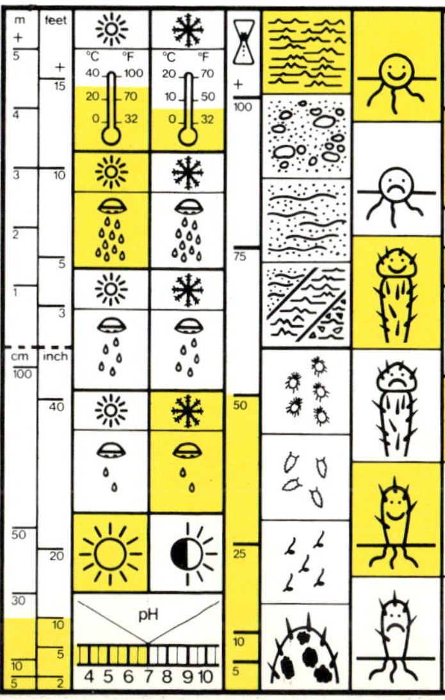

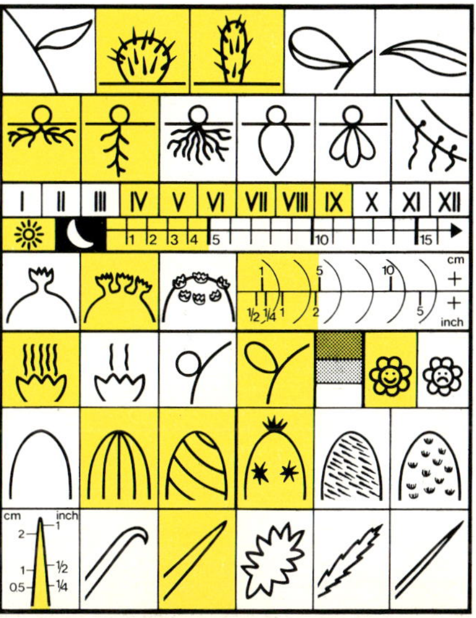

6

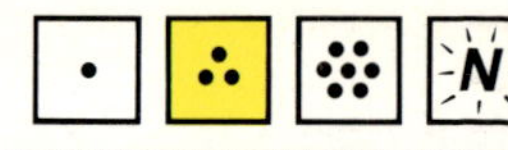

Echinopsis entrerios Don.
Argentina

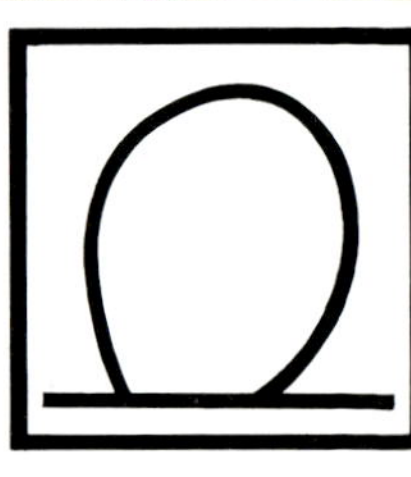

Echinopsis huotii (Cels.) Lab.
Bolivia

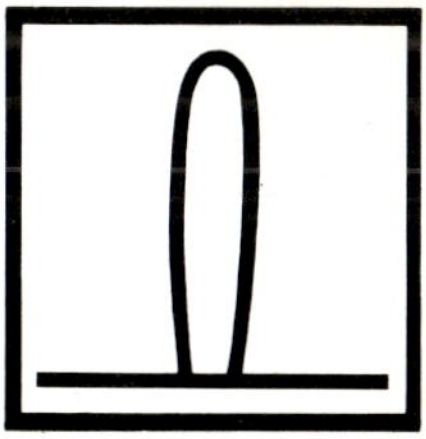

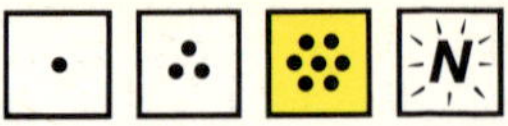

8

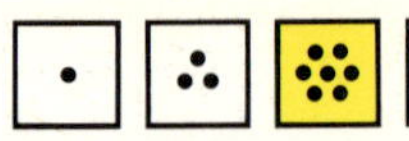

Eriocereus bonplandii (Parm.) Ricc.
Brazil, Argentina

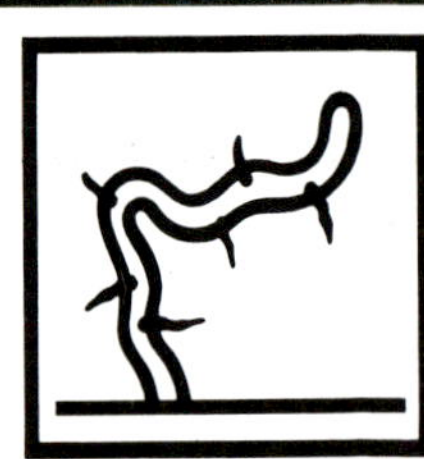

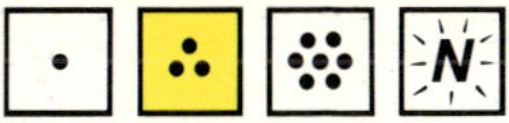

Gymnocalycium guerkeanum (Heese)
Br. & R.
Bolivia

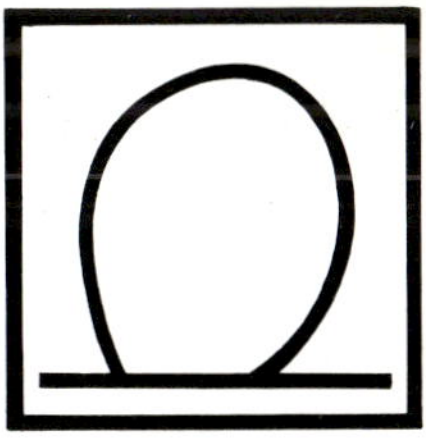

10

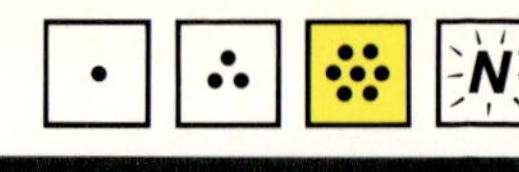

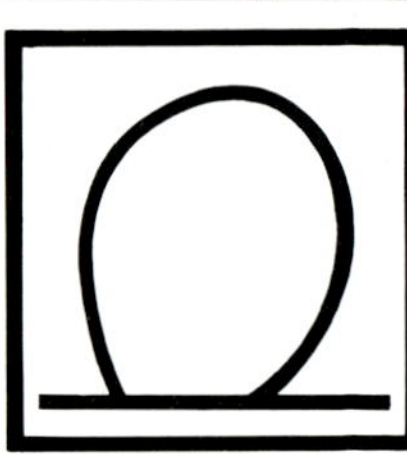

Gymnocalycium mihanovichii (Frič. & Gurke) Br. & R.
Paraguay

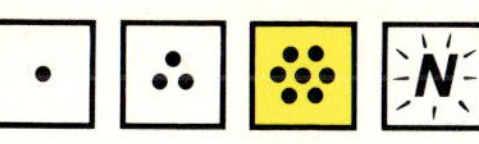

Leptocladodia microhelia Werd.
Mexico

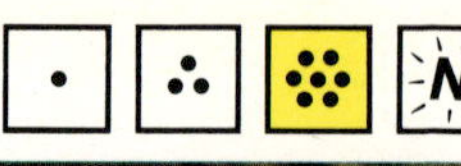

Mammillaria elongata DC.
Mexico

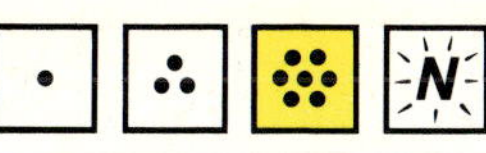

13

Mammillaria gracilis Pfeiff.
Mexico

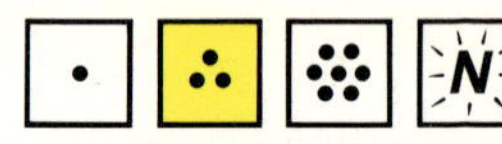

Mammillaria haehneliana Böd.
Mexico

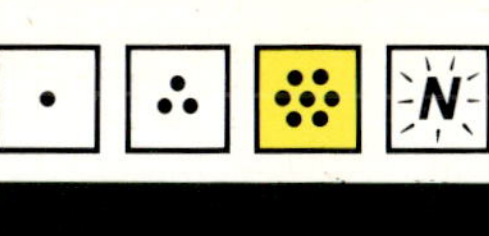

Mammillaria hirsuta Böd.
Mexico

16

Mammillaria leucantha Böd.
Mexico

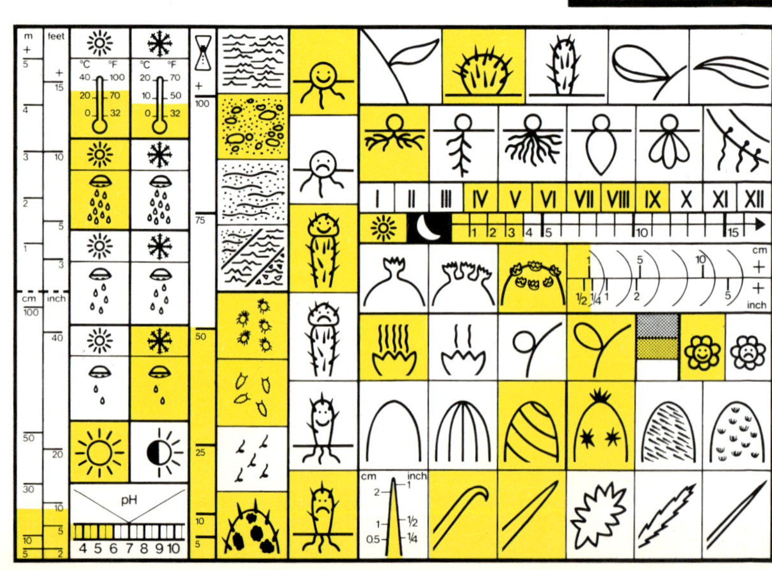

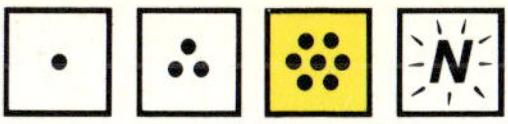

Monvillea speggazinii (Web.) Br. & R.
Paraguay

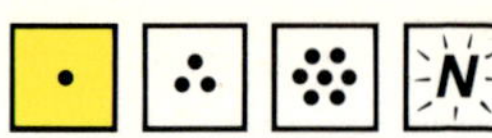

Neobesseya similis (Eng.) Br. & R.
[**Coryphantha missouriensis** var.
caespitosa (Engelmann) L. Benson]
USA

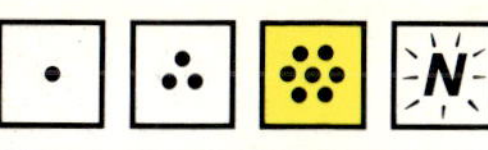

Neochilenia paucicostata (Ritt.) Backbg.
var. **viridis** (Ritt.) Backbg.
Chile

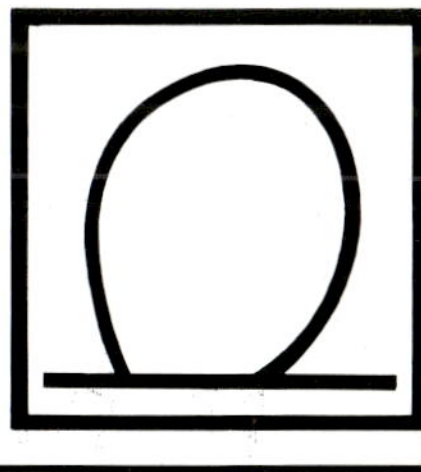

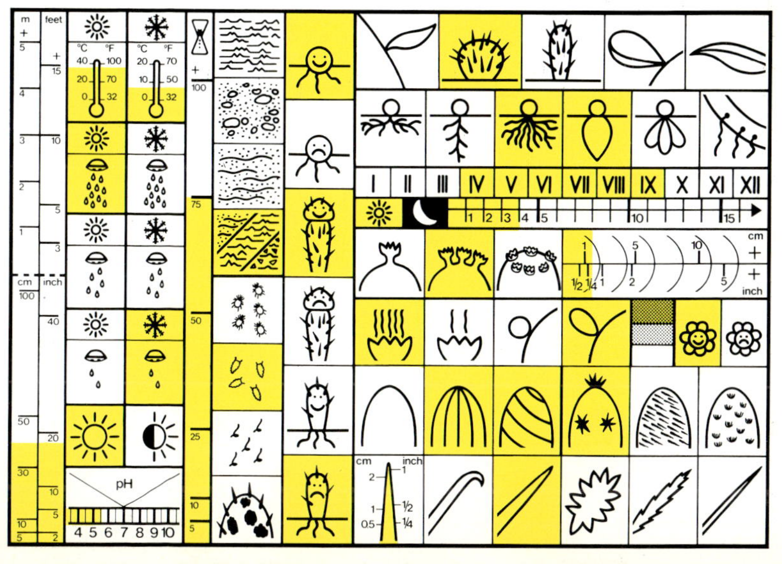

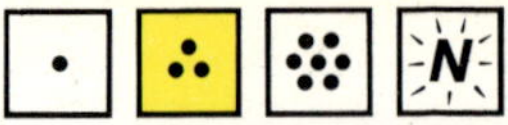

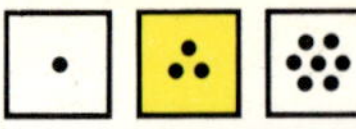

Nopalxochia ackermanii (Haw.) Knuth
Mexico

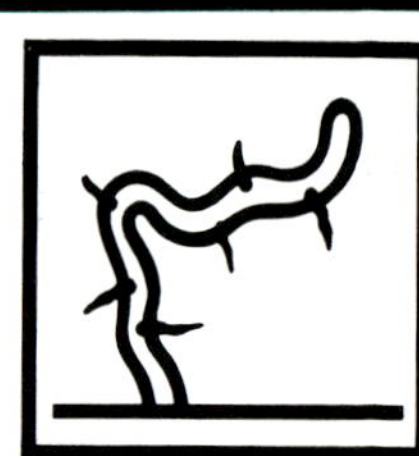

Pfeiffera yantothele (Morv.) Web.
Bolivia, Argentina

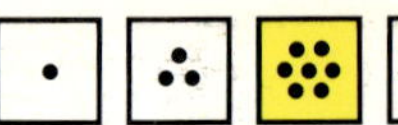

Pseudolobivia leucorhodantha (Backbg.) Backbg.
Argentina

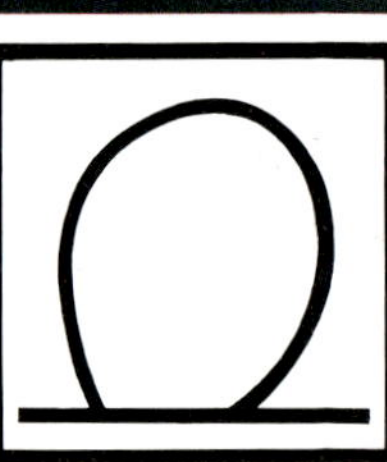

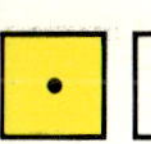

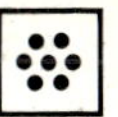

Rebutia albiflora Krainz
Bolivia

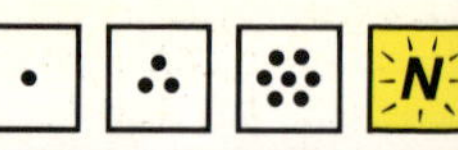

Rhipsalis rauhiaurum Barl.
Bolivia

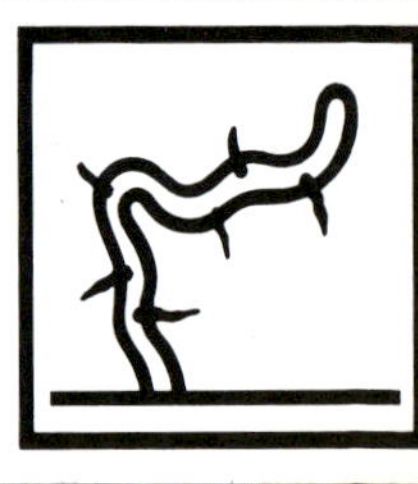

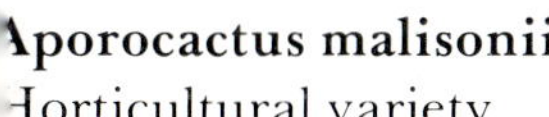

Aporocactus malisonii
Horticultural variety

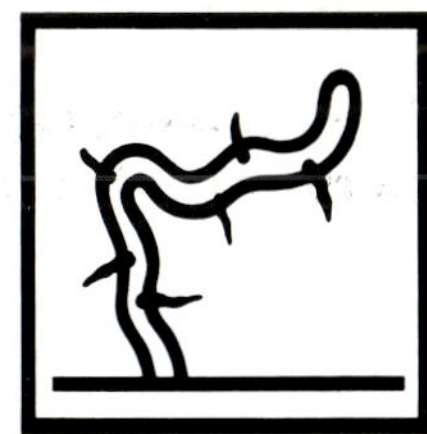

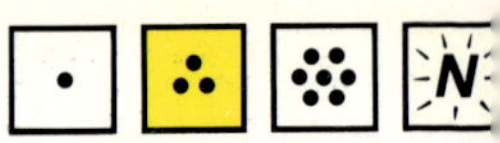

Aporophyllum celestinae

Horticultural variety

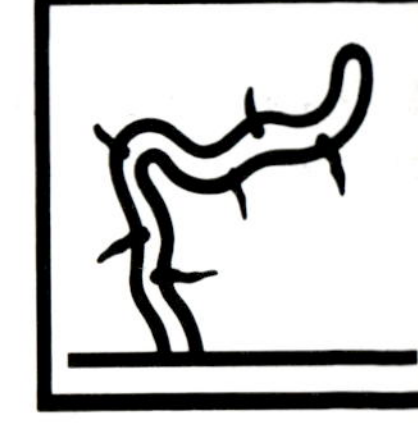

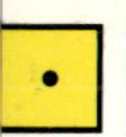   

Aylostera cajacensis Don.
Bolivia

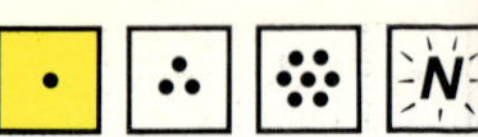

Aylostera coarctata Don.
Argentina

Aylostera kupperana (Böd.) Backbg.
Bolivia

30

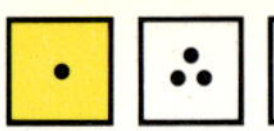
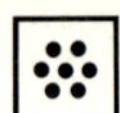

Aylostera mamillosa Don.
Argentina

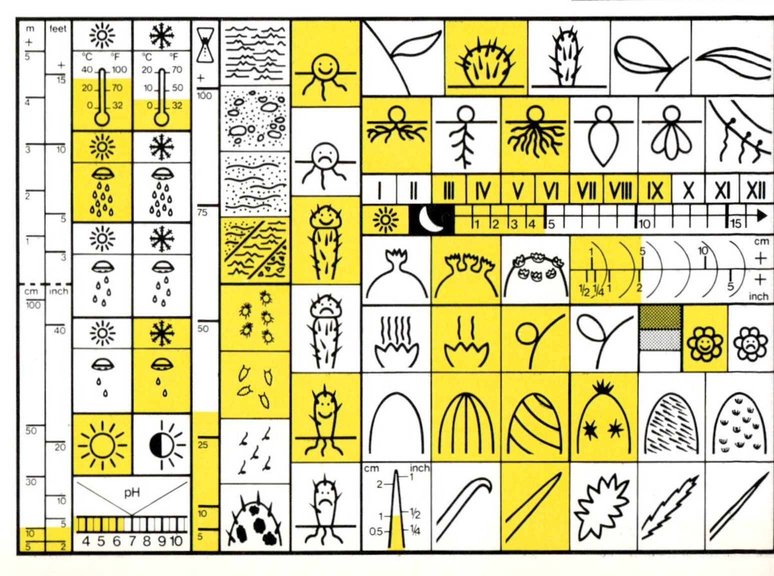

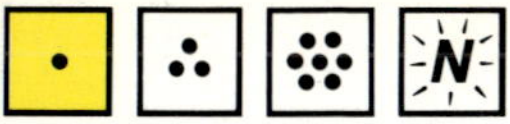

31

Aylostera pseudodeminuta (Backbg.) Backbg.
Argentina

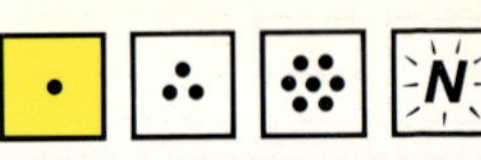

Aylostera pulvinosa (Ritt. & Buin.)
Backbg.
Bolivia

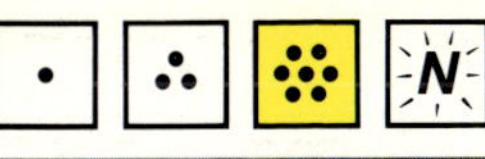

Aylostera spegazinii (Backbg.) Backbg.
Argentina

34

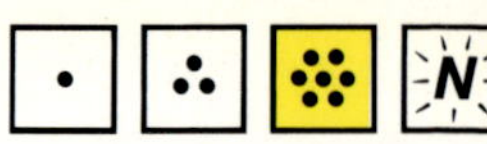

Chamaecereus sylvestrii (Speg.)
Br. & R. var. **aurea**
Horticultural variety

Cleistocactus tominensis (Wgt.) Backbg.
Bolivia

36

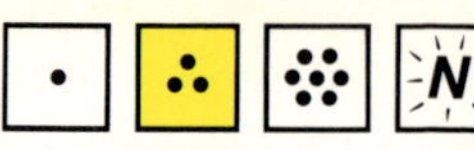

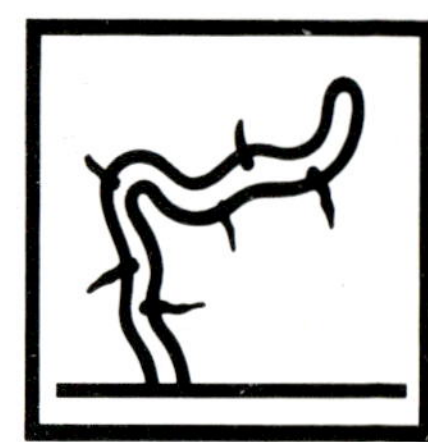

Epiphyllopsis gaertneri (Reg.) Berg.
Brazil

Gymnocalycium mihanovichii (Frič. & Gurke) Br. & R.
var. **friedrichii** Werd. Cv. **rubra** (Hybotan)

This is not a flower but a plant without chlorophyll. It cannot survive unless grafted onto stock capable of carrying out the photosynthetic process for both plants.

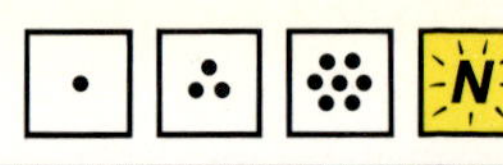

Lobivia ayacuchensis Knize
Peru

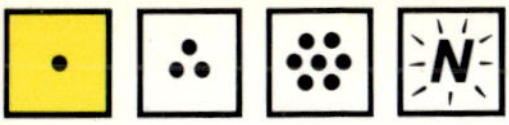

Lobivia bruneorosea Backbg.
Bolivia

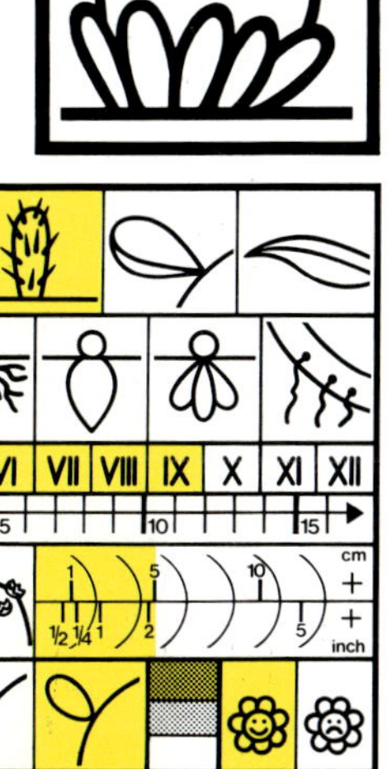

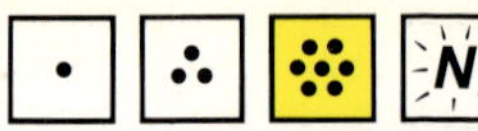

Lobivia hastifera Werd.
Argentina

Lobivia maximiliana (Heyd.) Backbg.
var. **caespitosa** (J-A. Purp.) Br. & R.
Bolivia

42

Lobivia maximiliana (Heyd.) Backbg.
var. **westii** Hutch.
Peru

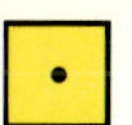
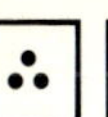
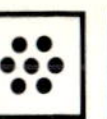

Lobivia sanguiniflora Cv. **cristata**
Horticultural variety

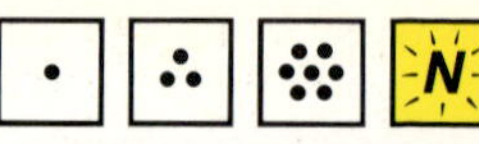

Lobivia sicuaniensis Knize
Peru

Mammillaria herreana Werd.
Mexico

Mammillaria kewensis Sd.
var. **craigiana** Schmoll.
Mexico

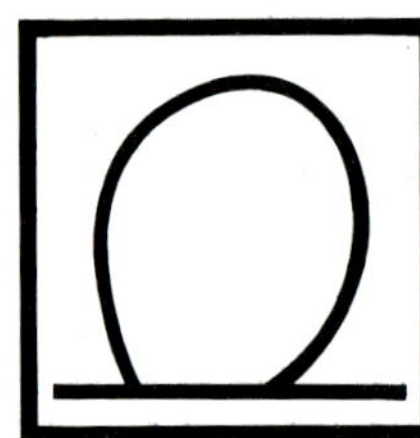

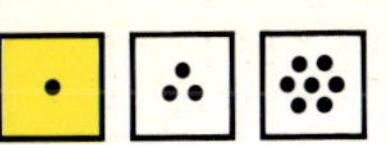

Mediolobivia nigricans (Wessn.) Krainz
Bolivia

48

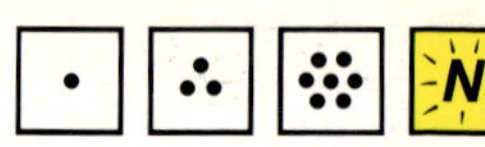

Rebutia buininingiana Don.
Argentina

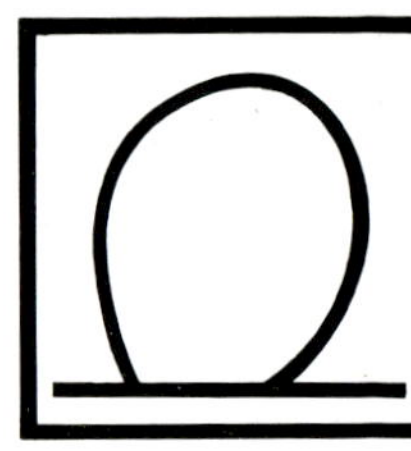

Rebutia gibbulosa
Horticultural variety

Rebutia krainziana Kesselb. Cv.
cristata
Horticultural variety

Rebutia residua Knize
Bolivia

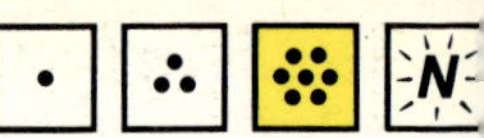

Rebutia senilis Backbg.
Argentina

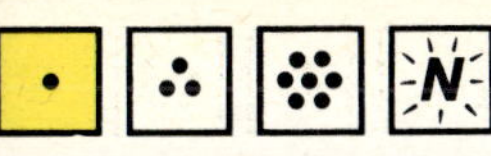

Submatucana madisoniorum (Hut.) Backbg.
Peru

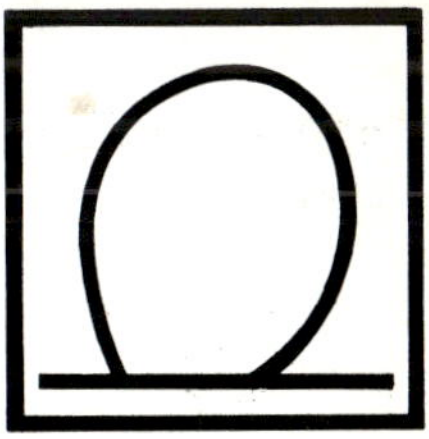

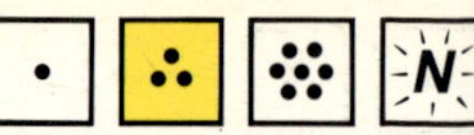

Submatucana paucicostata (Ritt.)
Backbg.
Peru

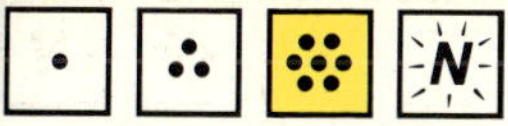

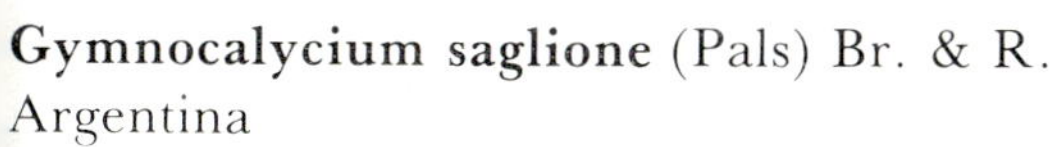

Gymnocalycium saglione (Pals) Br. & R.
Argentina

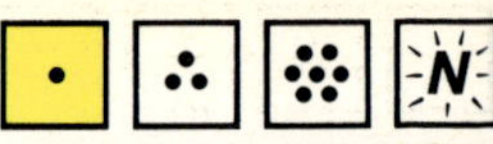

Lobivia chilensis Knize
Chile

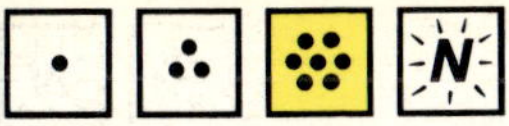

Lobivia leucorhodon Backbg.
Bolivia

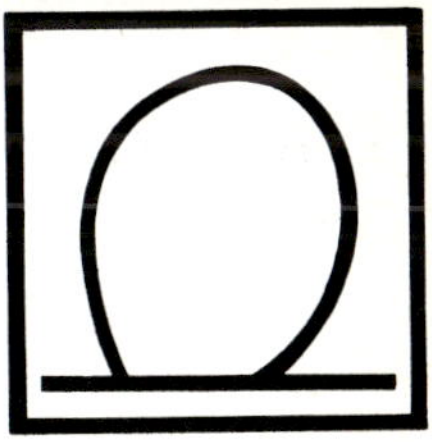

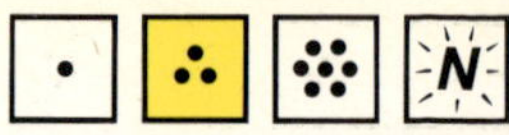

Lobivia oligotricha Cord.
Bolivia

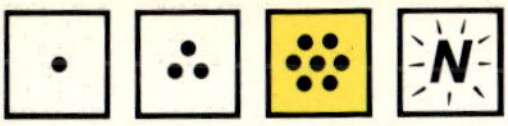

Lobivia pentlandii (Hook.) Br. & R.
Peru

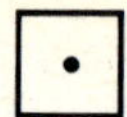

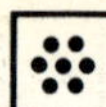

Lophophora williamsi (Lem. ex Sd.) Coult.
Mexico, USA

Named Peyotl by the Indians and used by them for its hallucinogenic properties.

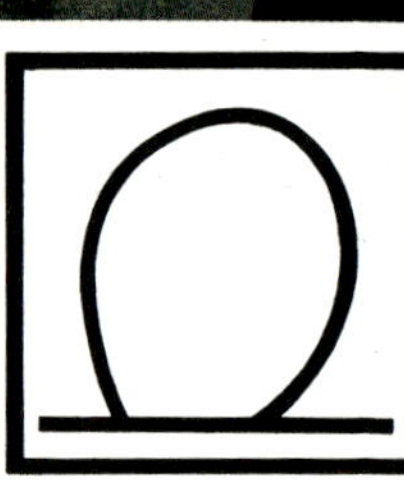

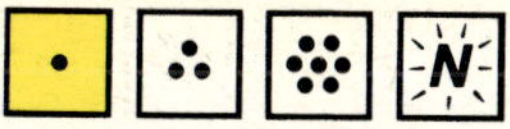

Mammillaria boolii Lindsay
Mexico

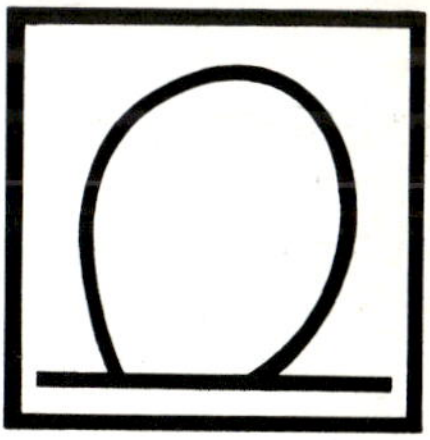

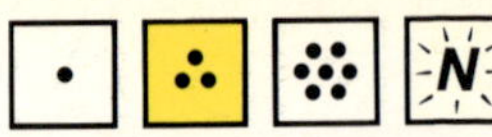

Mammillaria sheldonii (Br. & R.) Böd.
Mexico

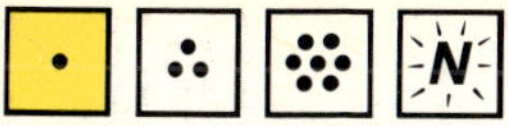

Obregonia denegrii Frič.
Mexico

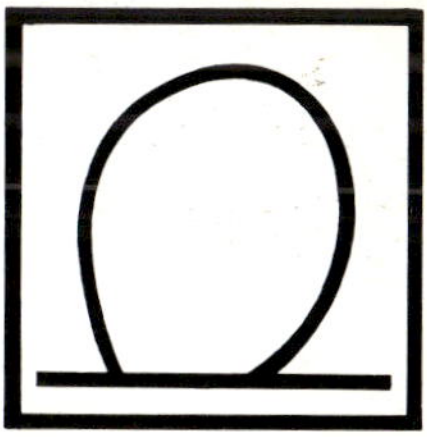

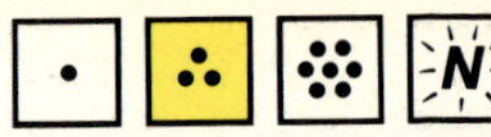

Opuntia basilaris Eng. & Big.
Mexico, USA

Several varieties, some endangered.

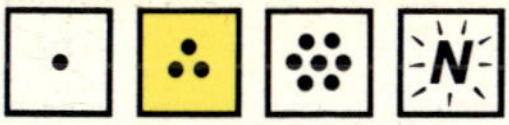

Pseudolobivia ferox (Br. & R.) Backbg.
Bolivia

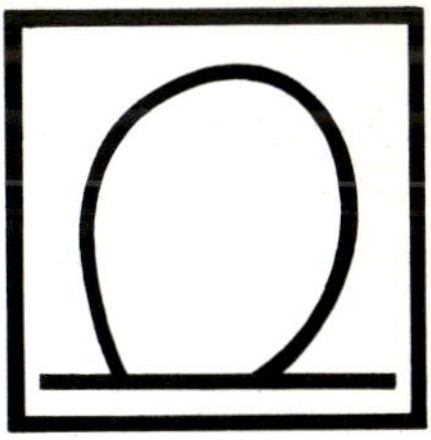

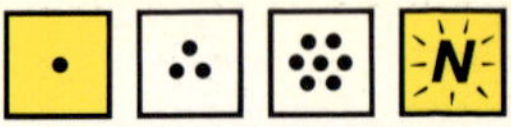

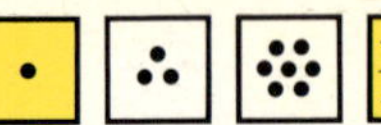

Rebutia espinosae Knize
Bolivia

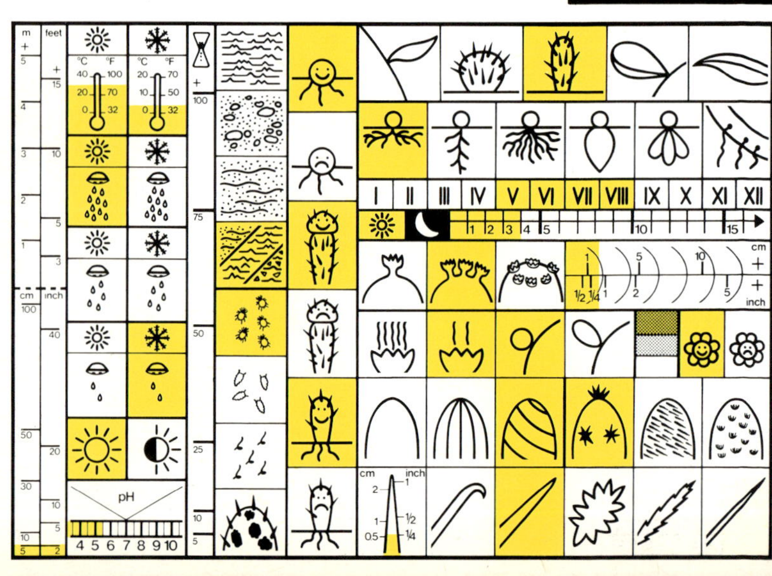

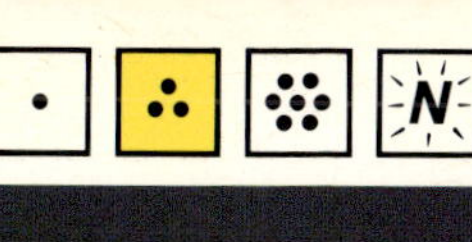

Rhipsalidopsis rosea (Lag.) Br. & R.
Brazil

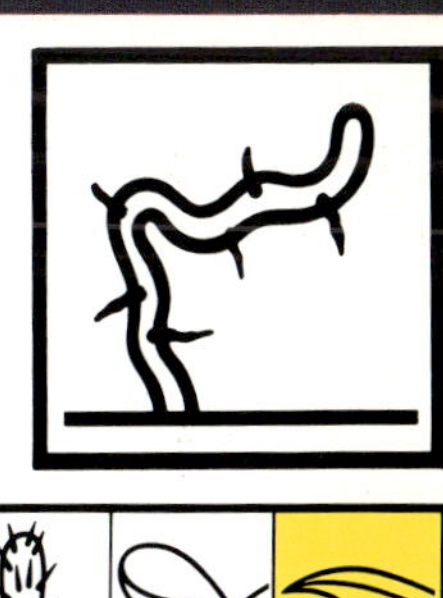

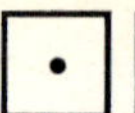

Rhipsalis rhombea (Sd.) Pfeiff.
Brazil

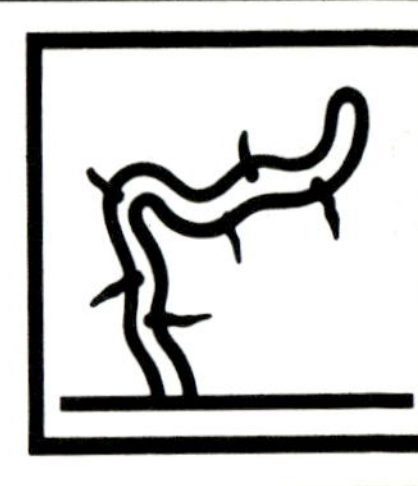

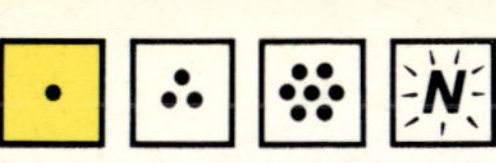

Turbinicarpus polaskii Backbg.
Mexico

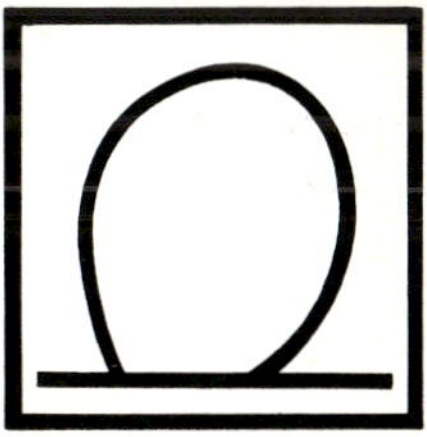

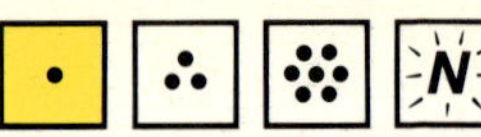

Acanthocalycium spiniflorum (K. Sch.) Backbg.
Argentina

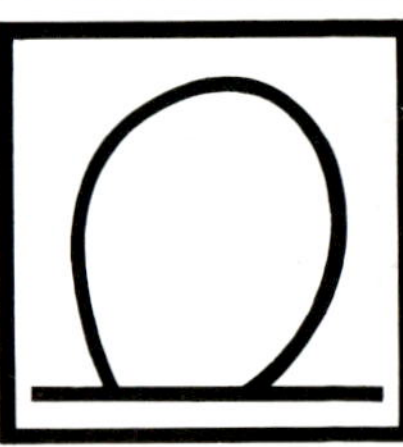

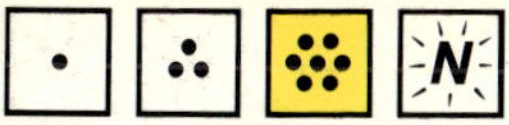

Acanthocalycium violaceum (Werd.) Backbg.
Argentina

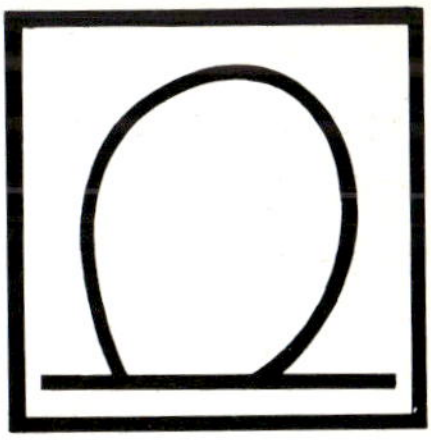

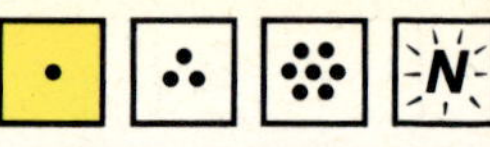

Arrojadoa penicillata (Gurke) Br. & R.
Brazil
Its fruits are unknown.

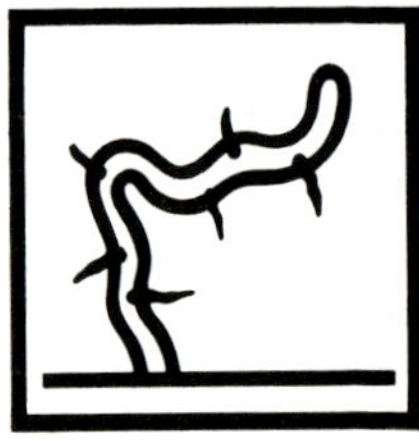

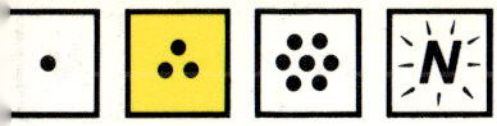

Echinocereus baileyi Rose
[**E. reichenbachii** var. **albispinus**
(Lahman) L. Benson]
USA

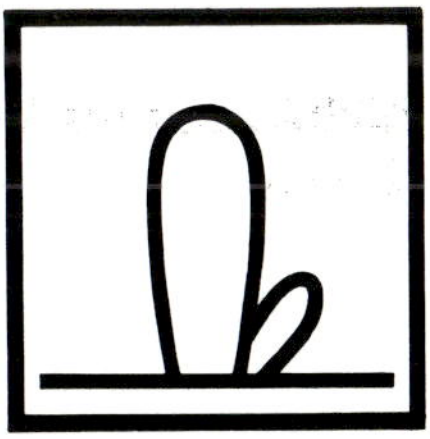

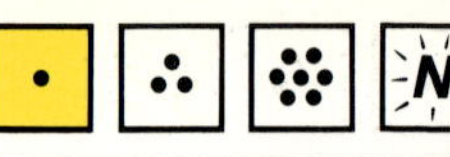

Echinocereus bristolii Marsch.
Mexico

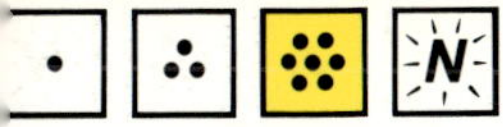

Echinocereus caespitosus Eng.
[**E. reichenbachii** var. **reichenbachii**]
Mexico, USA

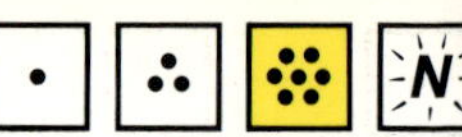

Echinocereus pectinatus (Schweidw.) Eng. [var. **rigidissimus** (Engelmann) Engelmann ex Rünysler]
Mexico, USA

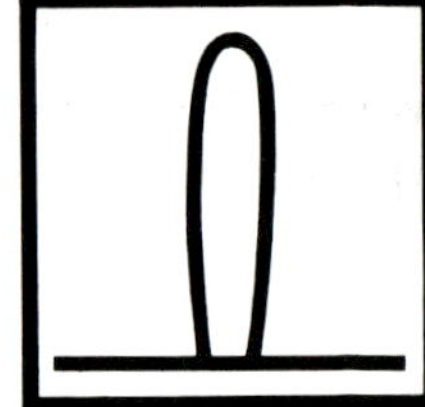

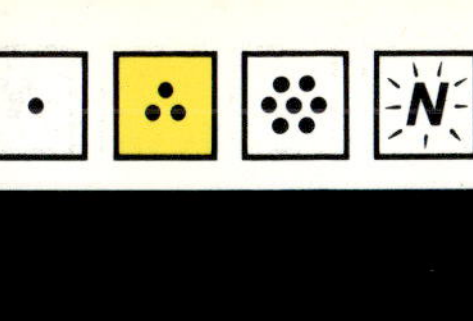

Mammillaria bravoae Craig
Mexico

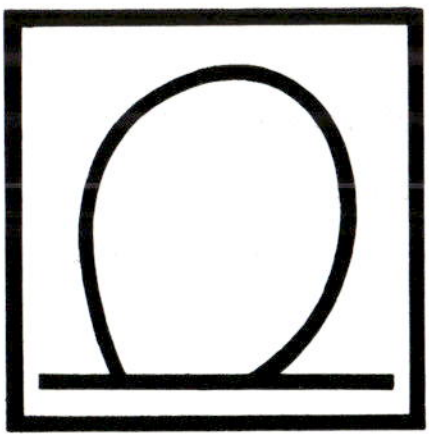

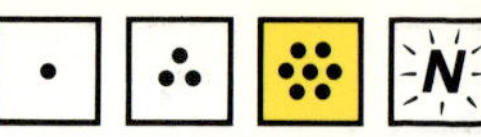

Mammillaria crocidata Lem.
Mexico

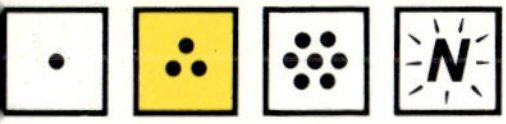

Mammillaria erythrocalyx Buchenau
Mexico

Mammillaria hahniana Werd.
Mexico

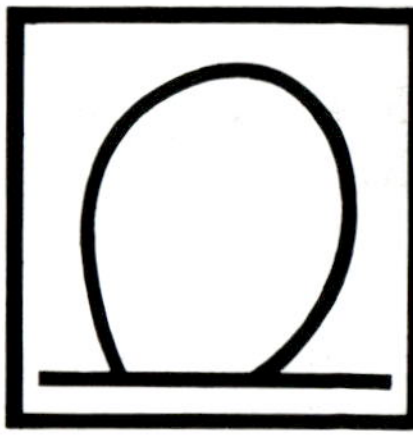

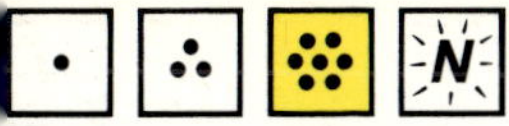

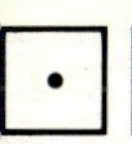
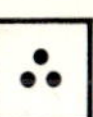

Mammillaria obscura Hildm.
Mexico

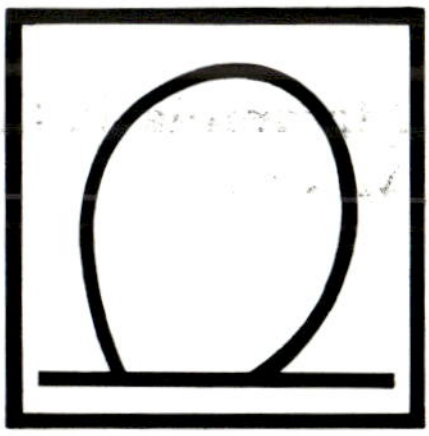

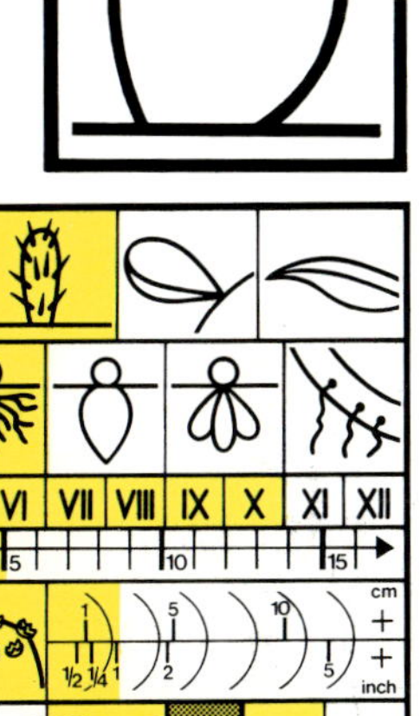

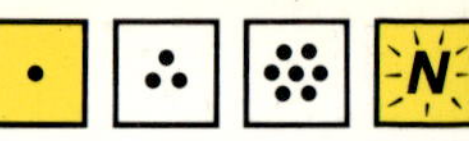

Mammillaria theresae Glass & Fost.
Mexico

Mammillaria wuthauniana Backbg.
Mexico

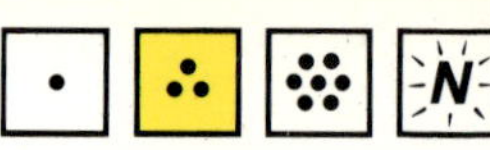

Notocactus herteri Werd.
Brazil

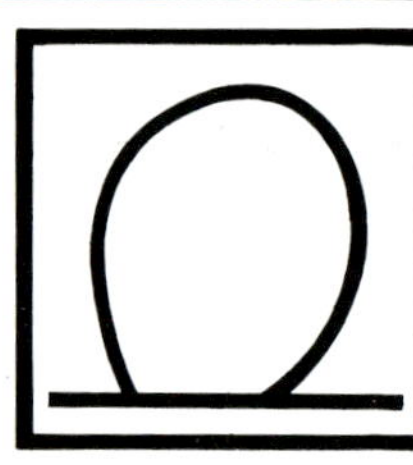

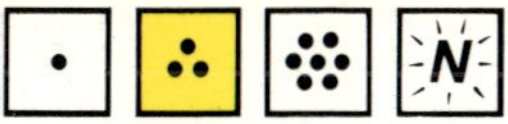

Sulcorebutia frankiana Rausch
Bolivia

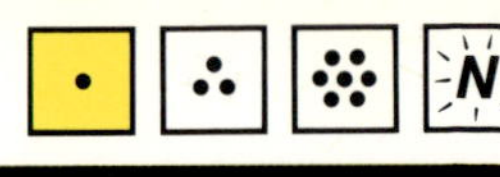

Sulcorebutia minima Frank
Bolivia

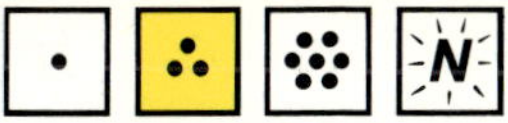

Sulcorebutia tiratensis (Card.) Rawe
Bolivia

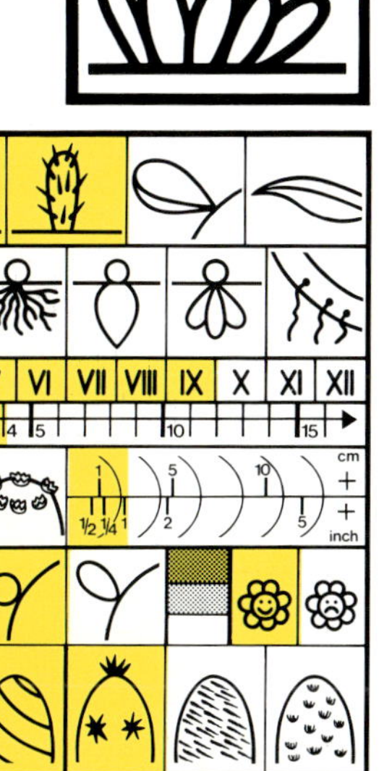

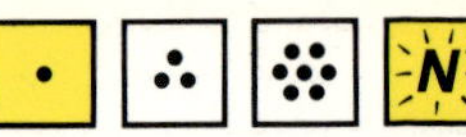

Sulcorebutia vazqueziana Rausch
Bolivia

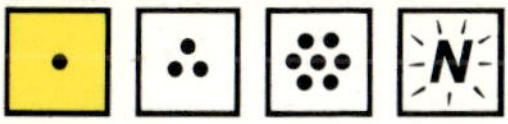

Weingartia crispata (Card.) Rawe
Bolivia

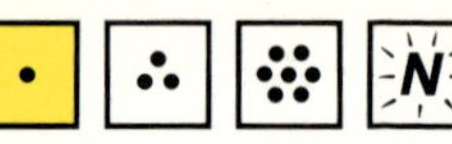

Delaetia woutersiana Backbg.
Chile

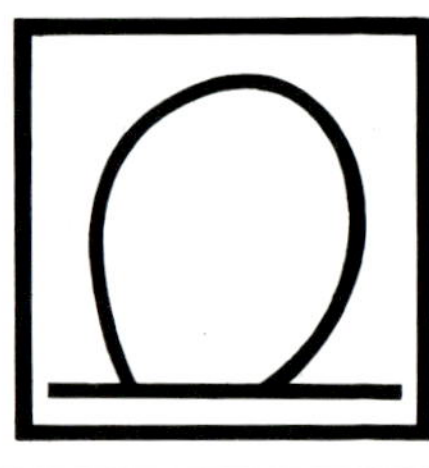

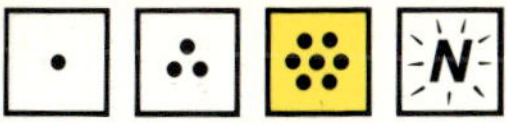

Echinocereus salm-dyckianus Scheer
Mexico

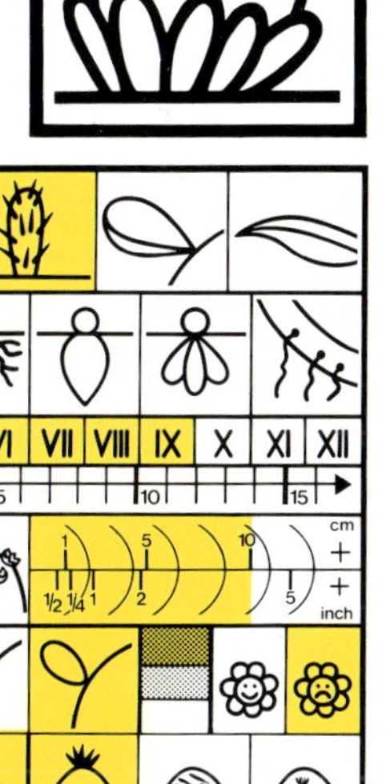

92

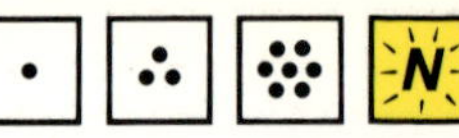

Echinopsis × Andeken & Frič.
Horticultural variety

Echinopsis × Delrue
Horticultural variety

m feet cm inch °C °F pH cm inch

I II III IV V VI VII VIII IX X XI XII

1 2 3 4 5 10 15

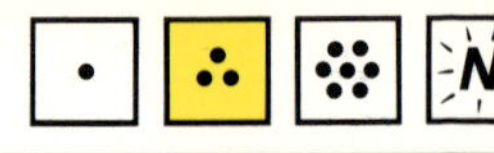

Echinopsis × Doinet
Horticultural variety

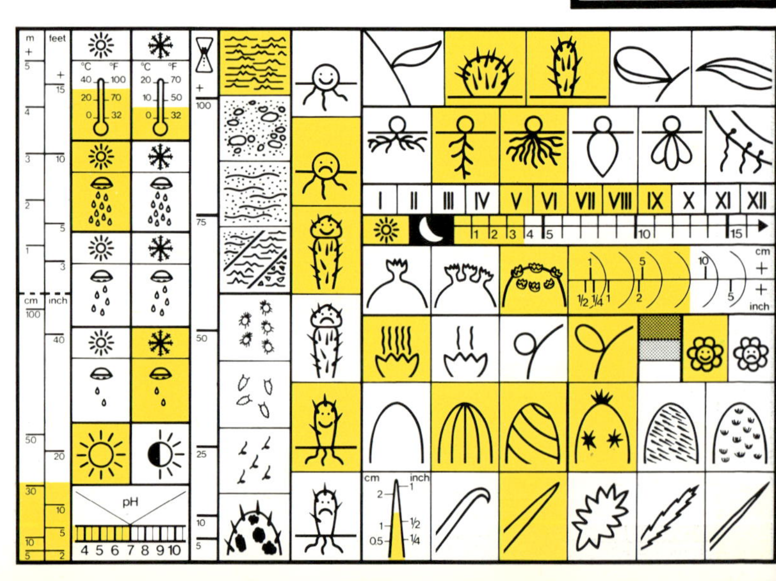

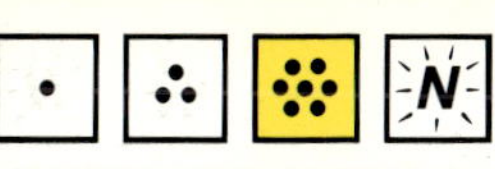

Echinopsis × Paramount
Horticultural variety

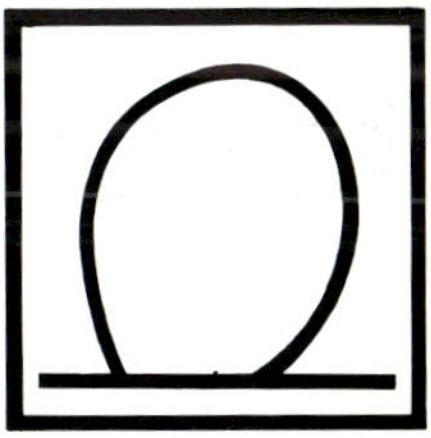

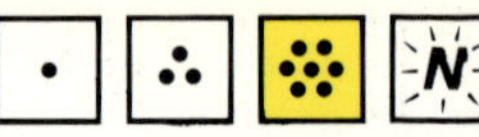

Lobivia famatimensis (Speg.) Br. & R.
var. **aurantiaca** (Backbg. et Wessn.)
Backbg.
Argentina

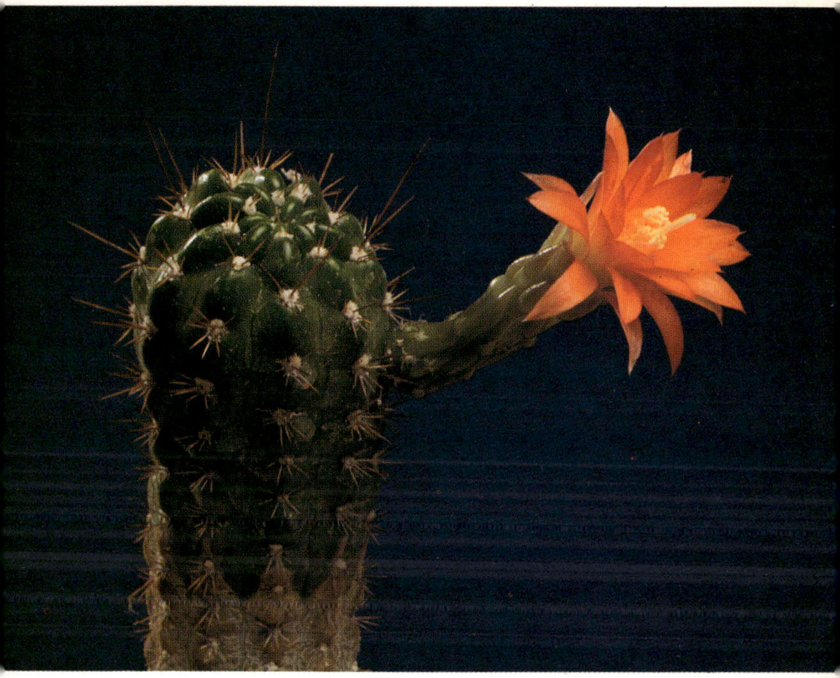

Lobivia maximiliana (Heyd) Backbg.
var. **hermaniana** Backbg.
Peru

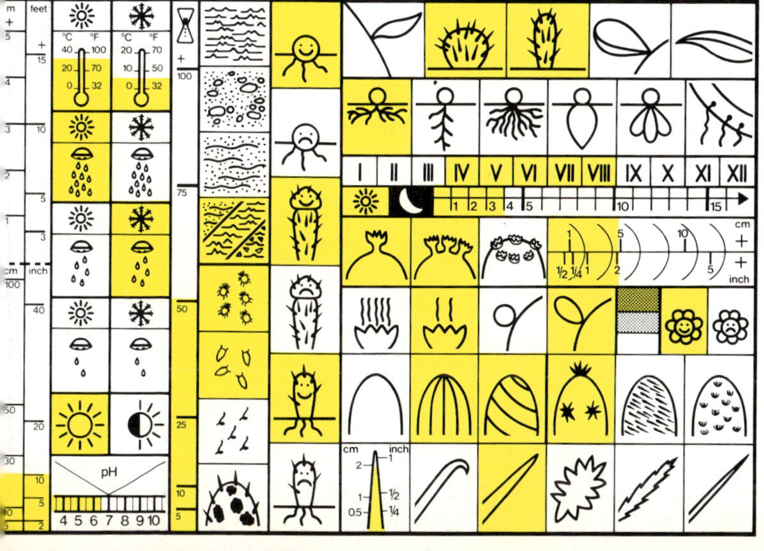

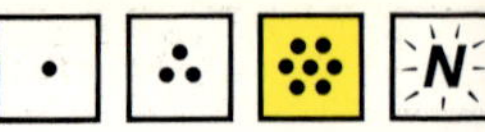

Lobivia polycephala Backbg.
Argentina

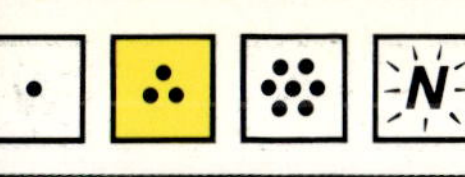

Mediolobivia pygmaea (Fries) Backbg.
Bolivia

100

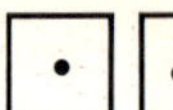

Opuntia ficus-indica (L.) Mill.
Mexico, USA

Grown horticulturally to rear Coccus (cochineal) insects and harvest its edible fruits (Mediterranean basin, Africa and southern Asia).

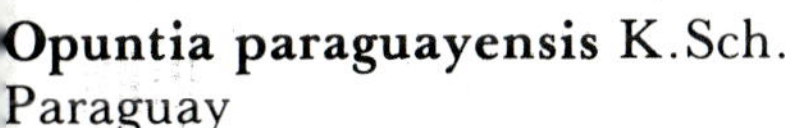

Opuntia paraguayensis K.Sch.
Paraguay

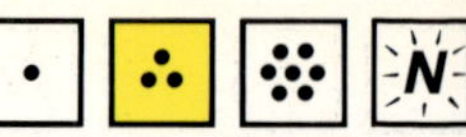

Parodia mairanana Card.
Bolivia

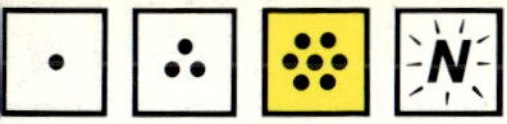

Rebutia hyalacantha (Backbg.) Backbg.
Argentina

104

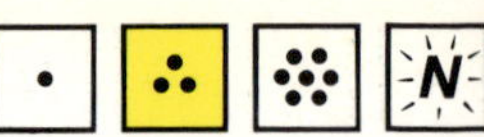

Rebutia senilis Backbg. **iseliniana**
Krainz
Argentina

Sulcorebutia tiraquensis (Card.) Rawe
Bolivia

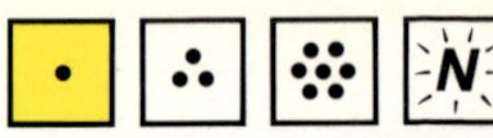

Winterocereus aureispinus (Ritt.) Backbg.
Bolivia

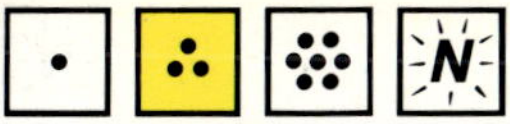

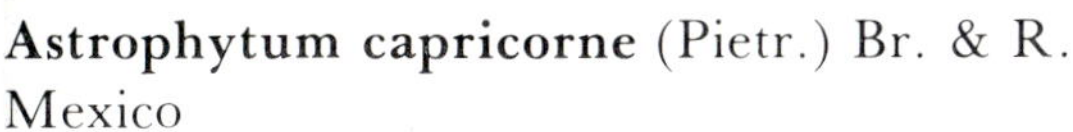

Astrophytum capricorne (Pietr.) Br. & R.
Mexico

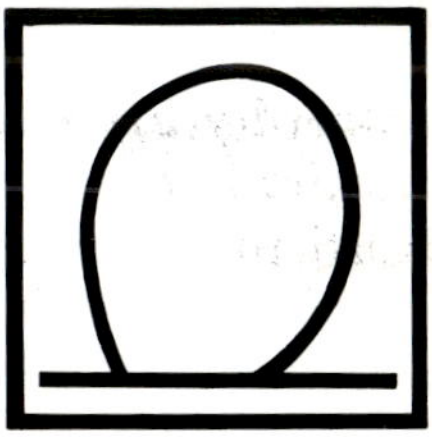

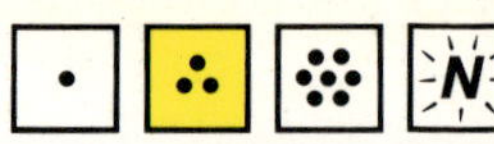

Astrophytum myriostigma Lem. Cv.
multicostata
Horticultural variety

Astrophytum ornatum (Dl.) Web.
Mexico

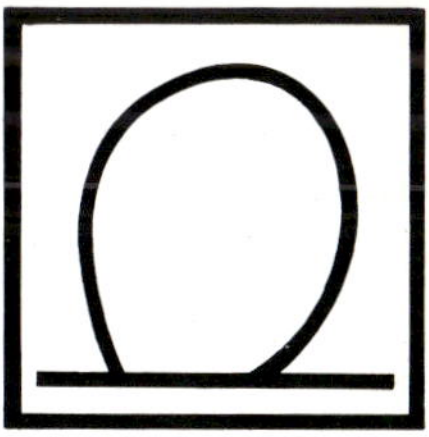

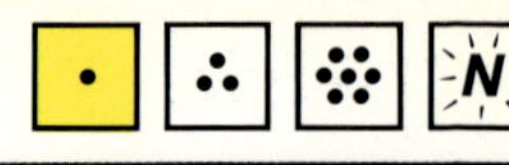

Cephaloclaristocactus ritterii Backbg.
Bolivia

Cephalocleistocactus pallidus Backbg.
Bolivia

112

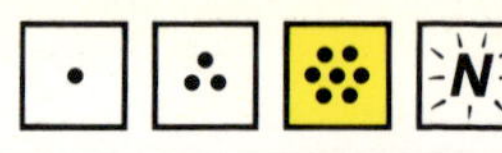

Dolichothele longimamma (Dl.) Br. & R.
[Mammillaria longimamma var.
longimamma]
Mexico

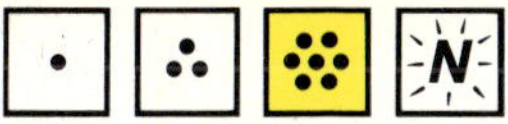

Echinocactus grusonii Hildm.
Mexico

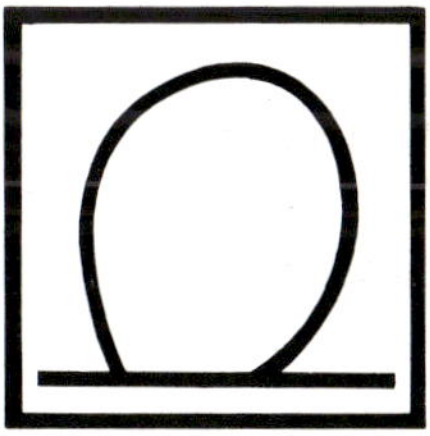

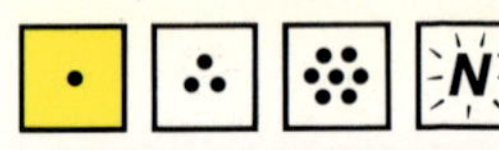

Echinocereus ochoterenae Orteg.
Mexico

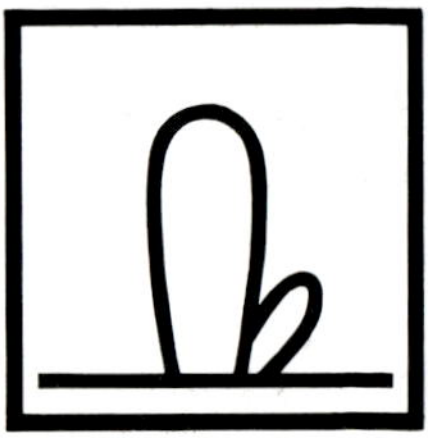

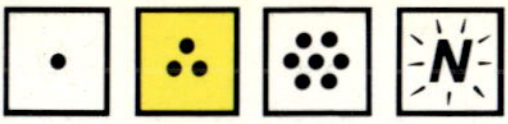

Echinocereus subinermis SD.
Mexico

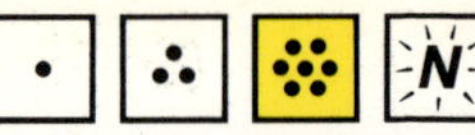

Eriocactus leninghausii (Hge-Jr.) Backbg.
Brazil

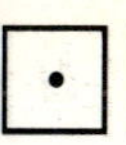   

Frailea itaberensis Buin. & Bred.
Brazil

These plants often reproduce themselves without the flowers opening, the seeds maturing within the fruits without pollination taking place (apomixis).

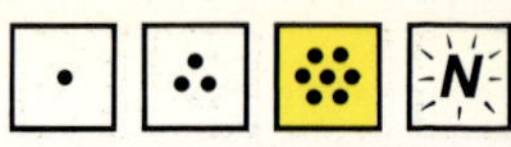

Hylocereus ocamponis (SD.) Br. & R.
Mexico

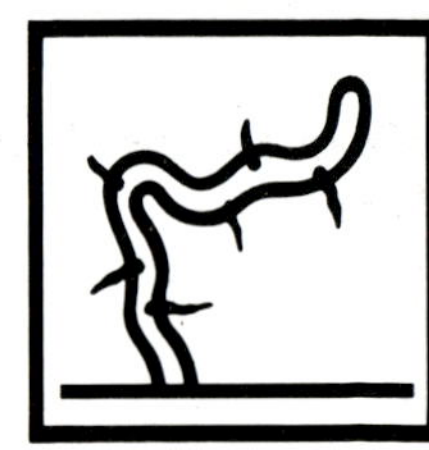

Islaya brevicylindrica Rauh & Backbg.
Peru

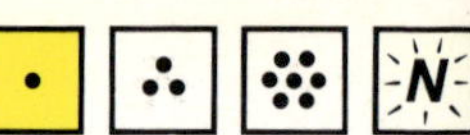

Islaya grandiflorens Rauh & Backbg.
Peru

Islaya unguispina Knize N.N.
Peru

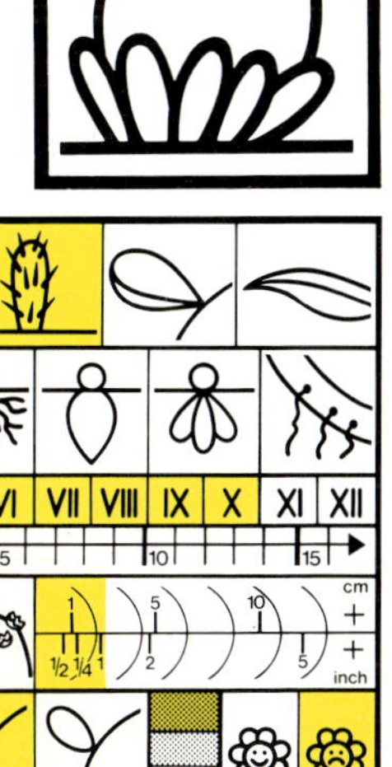

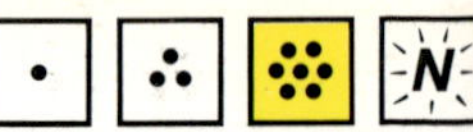

Lobivia cylindrica Backbg.
Argentina

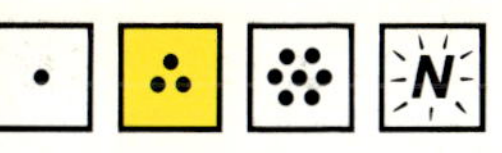

Lobivia scoparia Werd.
Argentina

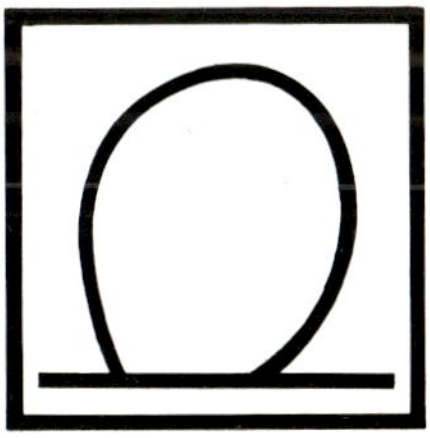

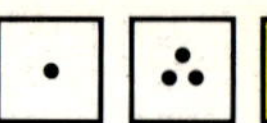

Lobivia varians Backbg.
Bolivia

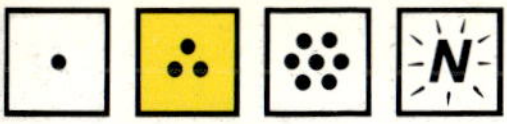

Mammillaria nana Backbg.
Mexico

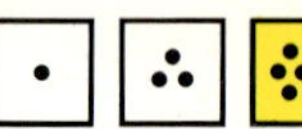

Mammillaria prolifera (Mill.) Haw.
Mexico, USA
[**M.p.** var. **texana** (Engelmann) Borg.]
Mexico, USA
[**M.p.** var. **prolifera**]
Cuba and Caribbean Islands – not native in USA.

Mammillaria wildii Pietr.
Mexico

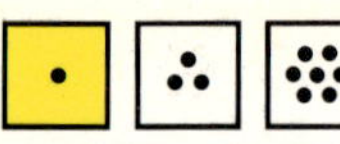

Mediolobivia euanthema (Backbg.)
Krainz
Bolivia

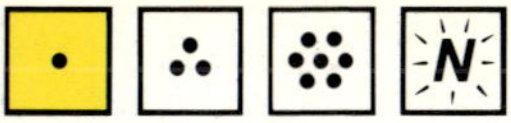

Neochilenia kunzei (Forst.) Backbg.
Chile

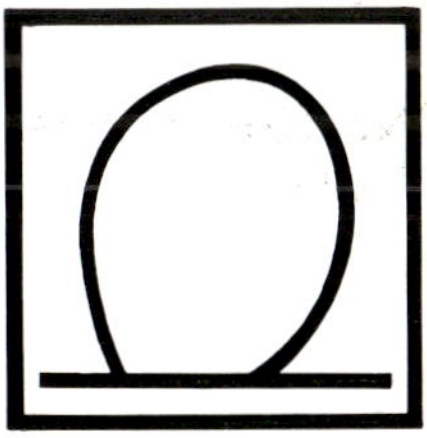

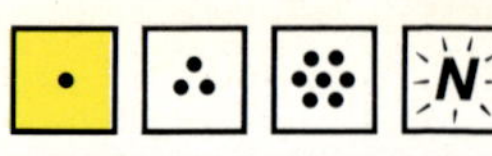

Neochilenia mitis (Phil.) Backbg.
Chile

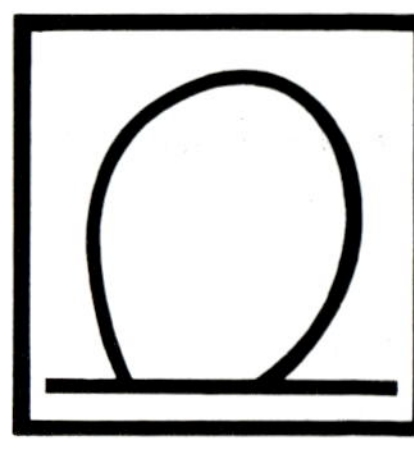

Notocactus ottonis (Lehm.) Berg.
Brazil

m	feet
5	15
4	
3	10
2	5
1	3

°C °F 40 100 20 70 0 32

°C °F 20 70 10 50 0 32

pH 4 5 6 7 8 9 10

I II III IV V VI VII VIII IX X XI XII

1 2 3 4 5 10 15

cm 1 5 10 + ½ ¼ 1 2 5 + inch

cm inch 2 1 1 ½ 0.5 ¼

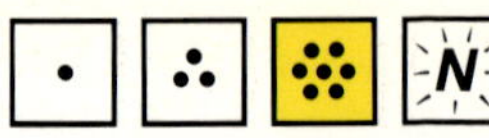

Notocactus tabularis (Cels. ex Schum.)
Berg.
Brazil

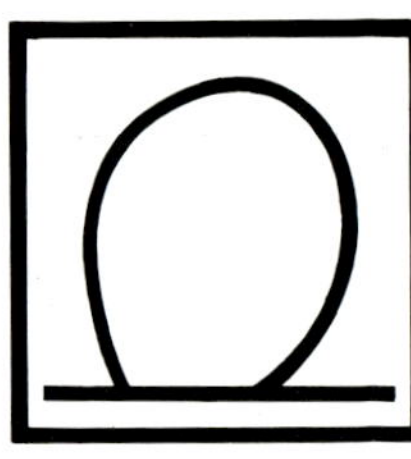

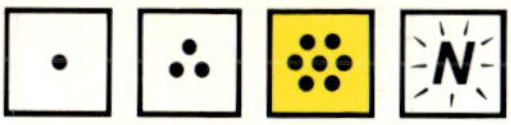

Parodia aureispina Backbg.
Argentina

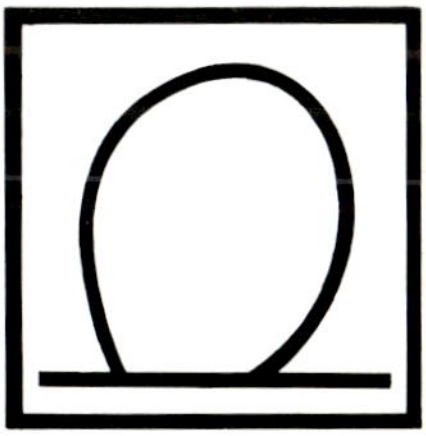

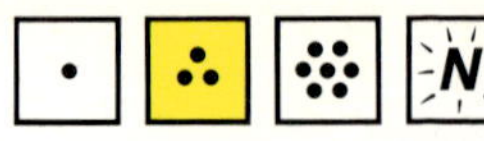

Parodia echinus Ritt.
Bolivia

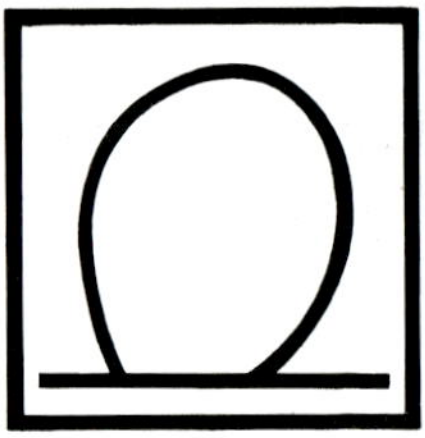

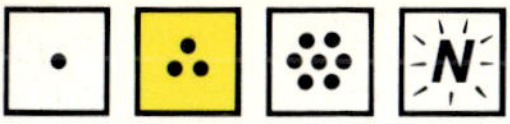

Parodia microsperma (Web.) Speg.
Argentina

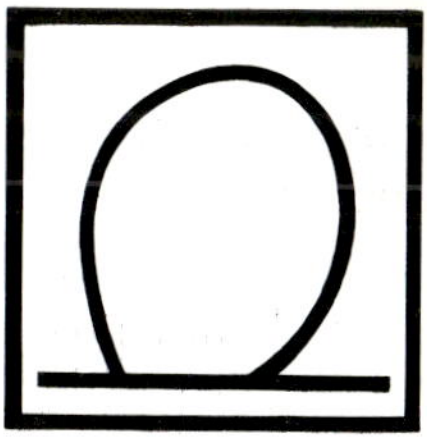

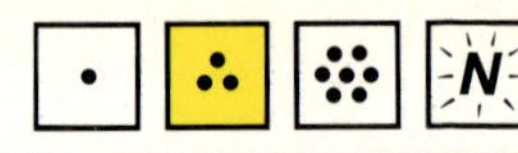

Parodia saint pieana Backbg.
Argentina

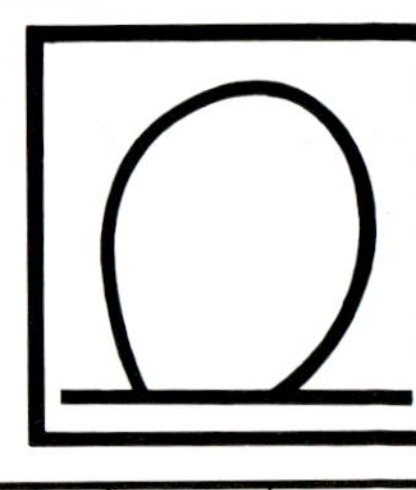

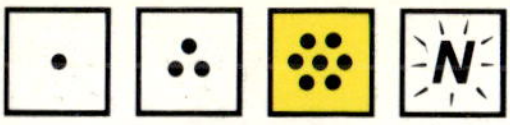

Pseudolobivia aurea (Br. & R.) Backbg.
Bolivia

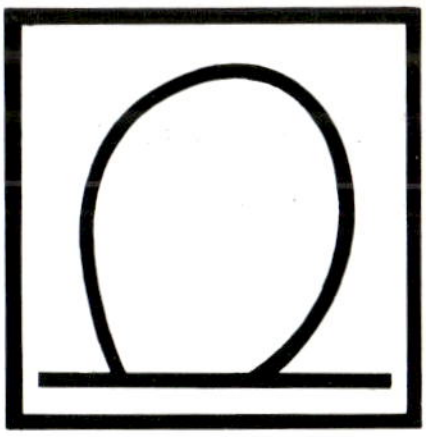

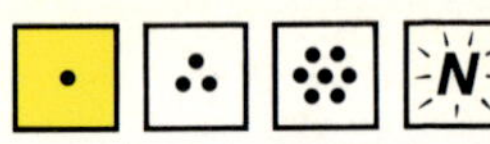

Sulcorebutia densiseta Rausch.
Bolivia

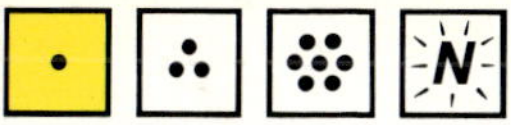

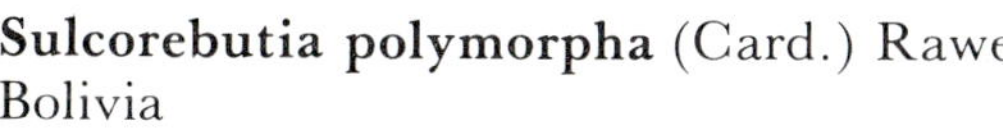

Sulcorebutia polymorpha (Card.) Rawe
Bolivia

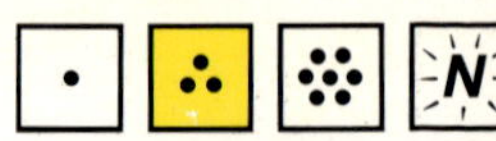

Weingartia breviflora (Backbg.) Rawe
Bolivia

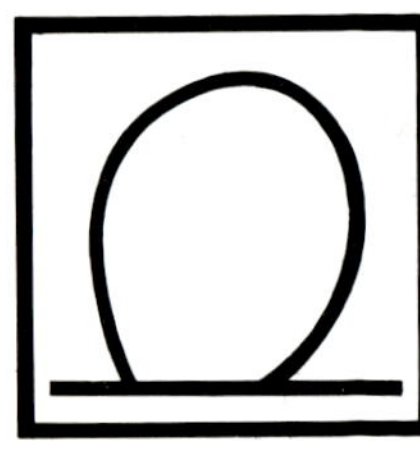

Weingartia pulquinensis Card.
Bolivia

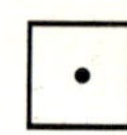

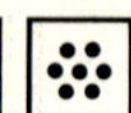

Weingartia vorwerkiana (Backbg.)
Werd.
Bolivia

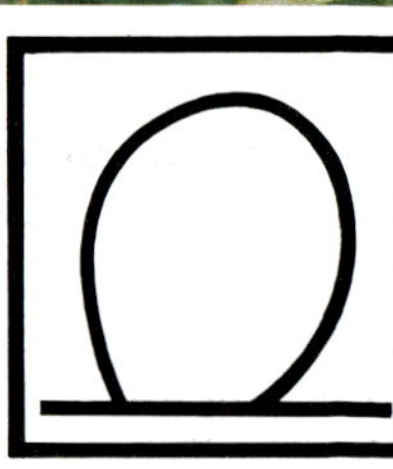

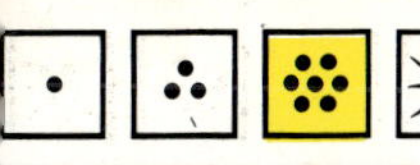

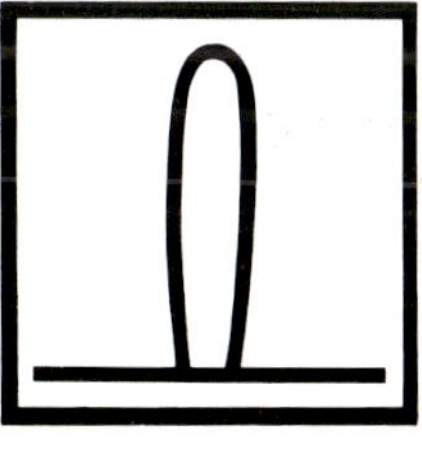

Austrocylindropuntia cylindrica
(Lamarck) Backbg. Cv. **cristata**
Horticultural variety

Cristate form, in which a deformation of the meristematic centre produces an irregular growth which never flowers.

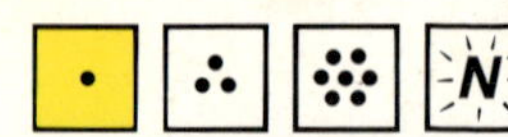

Cleistocactus viridialbastri Card.
Bolivia

HOW TO LEARN MORE ABOUT CACTI

FURTHER READING

Andersohn, Gunter, *Cacti and Succulents,* E.P. Publishing (1983)

Backenberg, C., *Cactus Lexicon,* Blandford Press (1978)

Barkhuisen, B.P., *Succulents of Southern Africa,* Purnell & Sons (1977)

Barthlott, W., *Cacti,* Stanley Thorns (1978)

Bechtel, H., *Cactus Identifier,* Oak Tree Press (1977)

Benson, Lyman, *The Cacti of Arizona,* 3rd ed, University of Arizona Press (1969)

——, *The Cacti of the United States and Canada,* Stanford University Press (1982)

Borg, J., *Cacti,* Blandford Press (1970)

Ginns, R., *Cacti and other Succulents,* David & Charles (1975)

Glass C. and Foster, R., *Cacti and Succulents for the Amateur,* Blandford Press (1976)

Innes, C., *The Complete Handbook of Cacti and Succulents,* Ward Lock (1977)

Lamb, Edgar and Lamp, Brian, *Pocket Encyclopedia of Cacti in Colour,* Blandford Press (1980)

Oudshorn, W., *Cacti and Succulents in Colour,* Lutterworth Press (1977)

Riha, J. and Subik, R., *The Illustrated Encyclopedia of Cacti and Other Succulents,* Octopus (1981)

Rowley, G., *The Illustrated Encyclopaedia of Succulents,* Salamander Books (1978)

COLLECTIONS TO VISIT

Austria

Linz: Botanischer Garten und Arboretum der Stadt Linz, Bancalariweg, 41-A/4020 Linz.

Vienna: Botanischer Garten der Universität Wien, Wien III, Renweg 14.

Belgium

Liège: Jardin Botanique de l'Université, rue Fusch, 3-4000-Liège.

France

Eze-sur-Mer: Jardin Exotique d'Eze-sur-Mer, Alpes Maritimes.

Paris: Museum d'Histoire Naturelle, rue Buffon, Paris.

Saint Jean-Cap Ferrat: Les Cèdres, 06290 Saint Jean-Cap Ferrat, Alpes Maritimes. This garden contains the valuable collections amassed by the late M. Marnier-Lapostolle, the great amateur botanist. Previous written application to visit essential.

Sanary-sur-Mer: Jardin Exotique de Sanary-sur-Mer, Var.

Germany

Frankfurt am Main: Palmengarten, Frankfurt am Main.

Munich: Botanischer Garten München, Menzingerstrasse 63, München 19.

Great Britain

Kew: Royal Botanic Gardens, Kew, Richmond, Surrey TW9 3AE.

Monaco

Monte Carlo: Jardin Exotique de Monaco, BP 105, Monte Carlo, Monaco.

Netherlands

Dronten: Fondation Flevohof, Postbus 40, 8250 AA, Dronten.

Spain

Blanes: Jardin de Acclimatacion 'Pyna de Rosa', Blanes (Gerona), Costa Brava.

Switzerland

Zürich: Stadtische Sukkulentensammlung, Zürich, Mythequai 88, Zürich 2.

USA

Colombus: Pancho Villa State Park, Ohio.

Los Angeles: Huntington Library, Art Gallery and Botanical Gardens, 1151 Oxford Road, San Marino, California 91108.

Los Angeles: University of California at Los Angeles Botanical Garden, LeConte and 405 Hilgard Avenues, Los Angeles, California 90025.

Palm Springs: Living Desert Reserve, Portola Avenue, Palm Desert.

Palm Springs: Santa Barbara Botanic Garden, 1212 Mission Canyon Road, ½ mile north of the old mission.

Phoenix: Boyce Thompson Southwestern Arboretum, POB AB, Superior.

Phoenix: Desert Botanical Garden, 6400 E. McDowell Road, Phoenix, AZ 85010.

New York: Brooklyn Botanical Garden, 1000 Washington Avenue, Brooklyn.

New York: New York Botanical Garden, Bronx Park, Southern Boulevard, Bronx.

ADDRESSES OF GROWERS

Most of the plants sold have been cultivated; only a few come directly from the wild.

Belgium

De Herdt, Rijkevorsel 2310.

France

Saint-Pie P., Asson 164800, Nay.

Germany

Dieter Andreae Kakteenkulturen, Postfach 3, Heringer Weg, D-6111 Otzberg-Lengfeld.

Köhres, G., Bahnstrasse 101, D-6106 Erzhausen, Darmstadt.

Schenkel, A., Blanckeneser Hauptstrasse 53a, D-2000 Hamburg.

Schleipfer, M., D-Neusäb bei Augsburg.

Uhlig-Kakteen, Lilienstrasse 5, D-7053 Kernen i. R.

Great Britain

Abbey Brook, Old Hackney Lane, Matlock, Derbyshire.

Exotic Collection, 16-18 Franklin Road, Worthing, Sussex BN13 2PQ.

Holly Gate Nurseries Ltd, Billingshurst Lane, Ashington, Sussex RH20 3BA.

Sargant, D. W., Hamperston Village, Wimborne, Dorset BH21 7LX.

Netherlands

Van Donkelaar, H., Laatje Ia, Werkendam.

Peru

Knize, K., PO Box 10248, Lima, Peru.

USA

Abbey Garden, 4620 Carpinteria Avenue, California 93013.

Grigsby Cactus Gardens, 2354 Bella Vista Drive, Vista, California 92083.

Hahn's Cactus Nursery, 2463 Loomis Drive, San José, California 95121

Henrietta's Nursery, 1345 N. Brawley, Fresno, California 93711.

Howard Wise, 3710 June Street, San Bernardino, California 92405.

International Succulent Institute, Corte Sombrita, 10 Arisula, California 94563.

K. & L. Cactus Nursery, 12712 Stockton Boulevard, Galt, California 95632.

Kimura International Inc, 18435 Rea Avenue, PO Box 327, Aromas, California 95004.

International Succulent Institute, Corte Sombrita, 10 Arisula, California 94563.

Loehman's Cactus Patch, 8014 Howe Street, PO Box 871, Paramount, California 90723.

Medlins Cactus Gardens, 2416 El Corto, Vista, California 92083.

New Mexico Cactus Research, PO Box 787, Belen, New Mexico 87002.

SOCIETIES' JOURNALS

British Cactus & Succulent Journal, published by the British Cactus and Succulent Society, UK.

Cactaceas y Succulentas Mexicanas, published by the Sociedad Mexicana de Cactologia, Mexico.

Kakteen und andere Sukkulenten, published by the Deutsche Gesellschafte, Germany.

INDEX

WILD HERBS: A FIELD GUIDE
J. de Sloover & M. Goosens

Whether used as a practical identification guide in the field, or for armchair browsing, this book offers a great deal of information succinctly presented. The herbs in the 144 stunning colour plates are grouped by colour. To identify a plant, simply open the guide at the pages bordered by the colour corresponding to that of the flower and you will soon find the plant itself. This ingenious system is time-saving, and the close proximity of illustrations of similarly coloured flowers helps to avoid misidentification.

For the purposes of this book, a herb is defined as a useful plant, one which is used to cure, to feed, to flavour dishes, to dye wool, or for any other specific aim. Pictograms presented alongside each colour plate summarise other properties – aromatic, medicinal and culinary, which parts are efficacious, when the herb is at its prime, where it grows, when it flowers. This at-a-glance information is supplemented by useful appendices, a glossary and notes on further reading.

MUSHROOMS & TOADSTOOLS: A COLOUR FIELD GUIDE
U. Nonis

Anyone interested in collecting mushrooms, whether to study them scientifically or simply to enrich their everyday diet with their nutritional value, will find this book an invaluable guide. It is based on a new descriptive system: each of the 168 colour photographs shows specimens in their natural habitat and is accompanied by a pictogram giving identification – at a glance – of their principal characteristics, combining a wealth of information with simplicity of presentation. Identification is further aided by the colours on the margins of the pages which reflect those of the fungi.

An introduction describes the main genera, their habitat, dangerous or valuable properties, and directions for collecting and growing them. Further Reading. Etymology of Scientific Terms and indexes contribute to the unique value of this guide.

MINERALS & GEMSTONES: AN IDENTIFICATION GUIDE
G. Brocardo

A completely new way to approach the mineral world is here offered to the experienced collector and the beginner. The 156 splendid colour photographs are accompanied by a brief description and a pictographic table which provides, through easily recognisable symbols, the available information necessary for identification and classification. The key to the symbols is printed on a bookmark. The margins of the pages are coloured to reflect those of the minerals themselves and aid quick identification.

The colour plates are preceded by extensive information on how to recognise and collect minerals, their origin and formation, their structure and properties, the classification, and how to prepare them for preservation. A glossary, bibliography and indexes complete the volume and add to its value as an indispensable guide for all collectors.

MOUNTAIN FLOWERS: A COLOUR FIELD GUIDE
S. Stefenelli

Thousands of enchanting flowers grow on the mountain slopes of Europe, and this book will prove an informative and useful guide for those wishing to discover more about them, appreciating their beauty and understanding the need for their conservation.

Recognition is easy with the aid of the 168 splendid colour photographs. To identify a flower, simply match the colour of the flower to the corresponding colour section and your task becomes easy. Once it has been clearly identified, the pictograms which accompany the plates will enable the beginner and the serious botanist to discover at a glance all the other interesting facts about the flower. A bookmark showing the key to the pictogram, a section on habitat, a glossary of pharmaceutical terminology, a bibliography and two indexes add to the value of the book.

FRESHWATER AQUARIUM FISH: A COLOUR GUIDE
J. P. Gosse

Fish, the most ancient vertebrates in the world, present an amazing diversity of form, colour and mode of life. New techniques for underwater exploration and means of transport and storage have fostered an ever-increasing knowledge of their ways and, with it, growing popularity for aquariums. Here you will find the answers to most of the questions you are likely to ask. Can the fish of your choice be placed in a tank where other species already thrive? What sort of food will it need? How does it reproduce? What temperature should the water be kept at? The answers are condensed in the pictograms which accompany each plate, these schematic little drawings, fully explained in the text, allow you to see at a glance what temperament and biological habit characterise your fish. The clarity of the 144 colour photographs is a precise guide to identification.

BUTTERFLIES: A COLOUR FIELD GUIDE
M. Devarenne

Many of the butterflies found in our gardens and our countryside are threatened by a hostile environment and the effects of pesticides and insecticides. The aim of this guide is to offer the reader a wealth of information about the different species, and by doing so encourage his interest in helping to conserve these 'winged jewels'.

Each species is photographed in colour in its natural environment, while a pictogram aids identification by detailing, in visual form, its major characteristics. An introduction gives a detailed explanation of the symbols used, information about the butterfly's life cycle and details of the characteristics of the different families. The text is complemented by a glossary, bibliography and index.

BIRDS OF EUROPE: A COLOUR FIELD GUIDE
L. Gonnissen & G. Mornie

Both beginners and experts will find this book an invaluable guide to bird identification. Learning the names of birds and discovering a variety of details regarding their habits is a fascinating hobby with several surprises in store. The task of identification and classification is made easier by the colour photographs of each species and their accompanying pictograms. These schematic drawings show at a glance the geographical distribution and biotope of the bird, together with its social behaviour, nesting and reproductive habits and the protection the species is offered by man. So often it is a bird's behaviour which identifies it from other species similar in appearance and the pictograms give instant clarification. The 144 species represented are all to be found in western Europe, some within the boundaries of gardens and public parks.

HOUSEPLANTS: A COLOUR GUIDE
L. Cretti & G. Barnabé Bosisio

Plants give interest and a lived-in atmosphere to every room, and brighten up porches, balconies and conservatories. Whilst certain houseplants are extremely hardy and thrive on minimal care and attention, others are more delicate and require a carefully controlled environment. The 144 colour illustrations included in the guide are accompanied by a brief description of each plant, providing precise details for identification and classification. A pictogram indicates the environment and type of care each one requires. A quick glance can provide information on the size of pot needed, light and humidity requirements, intensity and frequency of watering, methods of propagation and other useful tips. A bibliography and index complete this book which forms an indispensable guide for houseplant owners.

AMPHIBIANS OF EUROPE: A COLOUR FIELD GUIDE
D. Ballasina

Amphibians have a particular fascination. Their evolutionary role has been vital, providing the crucial link between aquatic life forms and terrestrial ones; today they play an important part in maintaining the delicate balance of nature. This guide includes all the species found in Europe. The 101 colour photographs illustrate the amphibians in their natural habitat and the accompanying pictograms provide information on appearance, classification, distribution and habits. In recent years there has been an alarming decline in European herpetofauna; this guide outlines the main threats and suggests practical measures for protection.